FUNNY
Business

Maple Tree Press Inc.

51 Front Street East, Suite 200, Toronto, Ontario M5E 1B3
www.mapletreepress.com

Distributed in Canada by Raincoast Books
9050 Shaughnessy Street, Vancouver, British Columbia V6P 6E5

Distributed in the United States by Publishers Group West
1700 Fourth Street, Berkeley, California 94710

Dedication

For Mom, who makes the best Flyface; for Dad, who always laughs at my jokes, no matter how stupid; for Jackie, who can still make me snort milk from my nose; for Karl, who still can crack me up with an oh-so clever pun; for Julie, who has made me laugh til my stomach hurt; for Michael, who gets funnier every day; and for Andrew, who is as nutty as his mom.

Cataloguing in Publication Data
Becker, Helaine, 1961–
      Funny business : clowning around, practical jokes, cool comedy, cartooning, and more…/ Helaine Becker ; Claudia Dávila, illustrator.

ISBN 1-897066-40-6 (bound).—ISBN 1-897066-41-4 (pbk.)

      1. Clowning—Juvenile literature. 2. Wit and humor—Juvenile literature. 3. Cartooning— Juvenile literature. I. Dávila, Claudia   II. Title.

PN6147.B42 2005   j791.3'3   C2005-901165-3

Design, art direction, & illustrations: Claudia Dávila

We acknowledge the financial support of the Canada Council for the Arts, the Ontario Arts Council, the Government of Canada through the Book Publishing Industry Development Program (BPIDP), and the Government of Ontario through the Ontario Media Development Corporation's Book Initiative for our publishing activities.

The activities in this book have been tested and are safe when conducted as instructed. The author and publisher accept no responsibility for any damage caused or sustained by the use or misuse of ideas or material featured in *Funny Business*.

Printed in Hong Kong

A   B   C   D   E   F

FUNNY
Business

Clowning Around, Practical Jokes,
Cool Comedy, Cartooning, and More...

WRITTEN BY
HELAINE BECKER

ILLUSTRATED BY
CLAUDIA DÁVILA

MAPLE
TREE
PRESS

CONTENTS

The Lowdown on Laughter

Stand-Up Comedy

Clowning Around

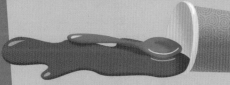

Practical Jokes

Comic Strips and Cartoons

Ready to Reel

Hold on to your ha-ha-hats, and let the hilarity begin! This book is full of *seriously* funny stuff. You'll find out how to craft a killer stand-up comedy routine, draw your own comic strips, clown around with the best of 'em, and even perform some gut-bustingly hysterical practical jokes!

What makes funny stuff so much fun anyway? People have been trying to figure that out forever. Here are some reasons you might burst out laughing!

WHAT A KLUTZ!

People like to laugh at others because it makes them **feel** better about themselves!

6

with Laughter?

People laugh **to release anxiety when there has been a big long buildup and they just *know* what's going to happen!**

People laugh at **things that are absurd, or things that don't belong together—like pigs in tuxedos!**

People laugh **when there's been a long buildup, they know what's going to happen, and—**surprise!** Something *else* happens!**

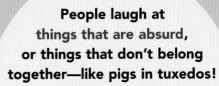

The simple truth is: **Funny stuff is fun because it's funny.** Funny people everywhere seem to agree.

Sight Gags

The Lowdown

Slapstick Humor

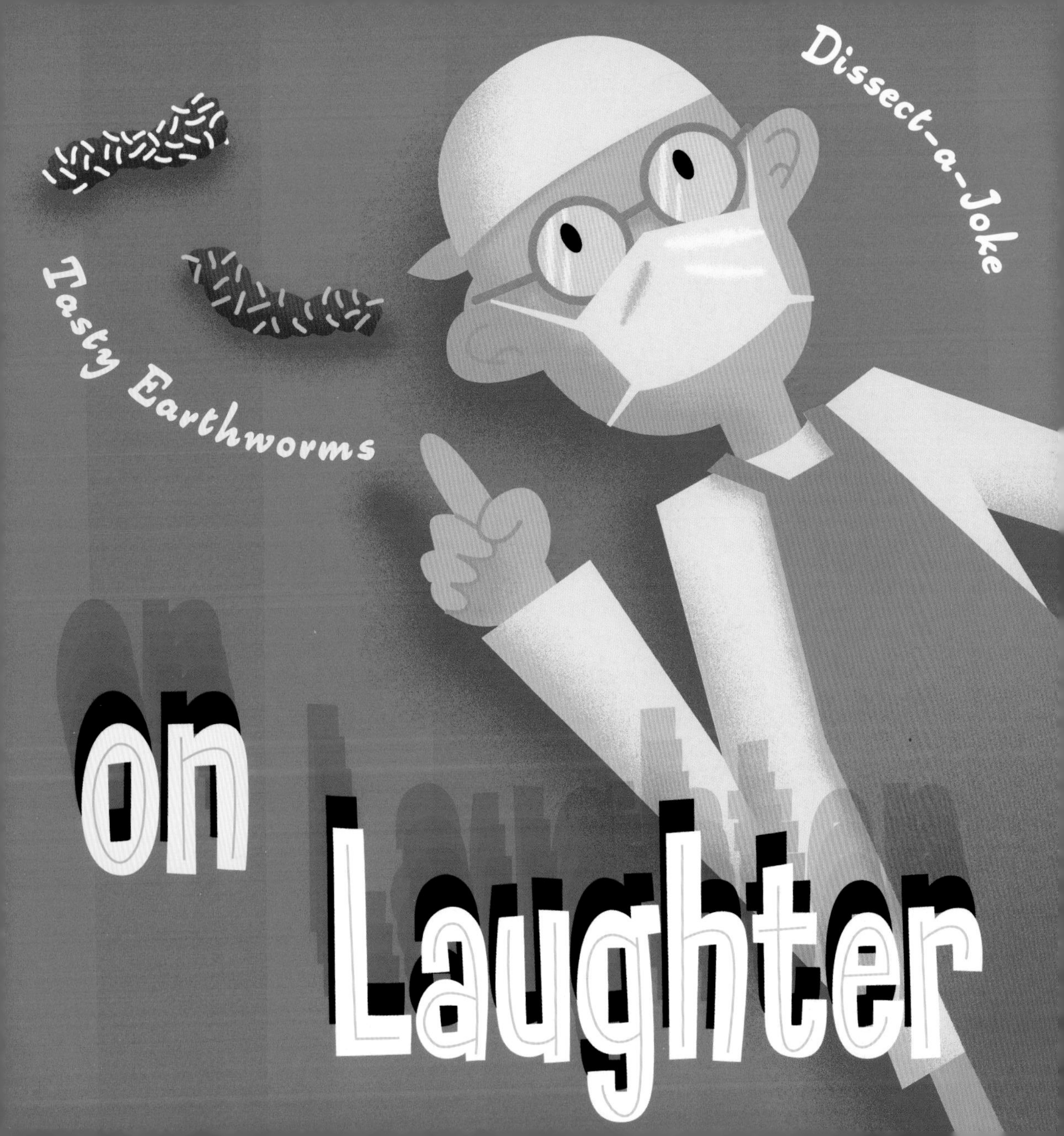
Dissect-a-Joke
Tasty Earthworms
on Laughter

Fabulously FUNNY Facts

Check out these strange-but-true stats:

- *Homo sapiens* (that's us!) is the only species with a true laugh.
- Most babies start to smile at around six weeks of age. The first laugh usually happens at four months.
- Most kids start making jokes when they're around six years old.
- On average, kids laugh about 400 times a day. Grownups laugh only 15 times a day.
- People speaking laugh 50% more often than the people listening to them.
- There's a link between yakking and yukking: the more talkative you are as a kid, the more likely you are to develop a great sense of humor.
- The word "humor" comes from a Latin word that means "fluid" or "moisture." In the 1400s and 1500s, people thought that we each had four basic body fluids, or "humors," that governed our health and temperament. To be "in good humor" meant that the four humors were all in balance.

10

Laughing is good for you! Here's why: when you start to laugh, your increased breathing and heart rate speed more oxygen to the rest of your body. Cell growth and repair increases, especially in your immune system. And as muscles throughout your body contract and relax, they get a terrific workout. The muscles also massage your organs, and help move food through your intestinal tract. Laughter stimulates thinking skills, creativity, and memory, too. It's true, you actually learn better if you are having fun!

ARE WE HAVING FUN YET?

FALLING DOWN LAUGHING

Did you ever laugh so hard that you practically collapsed? You're not alone. Scientific studies have shown that laughter almost totally blocks the "H-reflex," a brain signal that controls muscle tone. Your muscles go lax, and you literally "go weak in the knees." So next time you're in the Olympics, try not to laugh too hard before your big event.

FOLLOW

W ho says having fun is easy? Laughing is hard work! A good guffaw uses over 100 muscles, and 10 minutes of laughter burns as many calories as 100 strokes on a rowing machine. Check out what's going on in your body every time you laugh by following the diagram below.

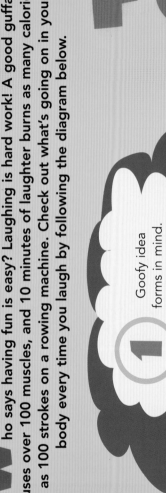

1 Goofy idea forms in mind.

2 The thinking parts of your brain become active.

3 Within seconds, regions of the brain linked with emotion and memory become active.

4 Muscles in the face contract. Diaphragm suddenly relaxes. Laughter begins to bubble up from your belly.

5 Breathing quickens. Heart rate and blood pressure speed up. Body temperature jumps.

6 Head tilts back. Larynx and epiglottis constrict. Laughter explodes in loud, rhythmic hee-haws from the mouth.

7 "Feel good" hormones called neuropeptides, endorphins, and enkephalins flood the body.

the LAUGH

8 Your immune system switches into high gear.

9 Eyes begin to water. Muscles throughout the body begin to convulse uncontrollably. Stomach and ribs begin to ache. You may have difficulty catching breath.

10 Intestines are squeeeeezed by stomach muscles.

11 Bursts of snorting, gasping, whooping, and drooling become more frequent.

12 Guffaws are gradually replaced by chuckles. Chuckles become giggles. Giggles dissolve into long sighs.

13 Laughter finally subsides, leaving you with a red face, drippy eyes, and a runny nose.

LAUGHTER IS GOOD MEDICINE

After a good bout of the giggles, your heart rate and blood pressure drop. Hormones are released that are both natural mood enhancers and painkillers. They make you more relaxed and they also reduce your sensitivity to pain. In other words, you feel great.

Dissect-a-Joke

There are a zillion kinds of jokes, but all jokes follow a similar pattern. To demonstrate what makes a joke funny, Dr. B. Hill-Arius, Director of the Institute of Seriously Funny Stuff, will now dissect a joke.

THIS IS ONE *SICK* JOKE!

Joke

Every joke has two main parts. The **setup** gives the information you need to "get" the joke. The **punch line** (a.k.a. the tag line, gag, payoff, capper, snapper, button, or blow-off) is the surprise twist at the end.

Setup: Did you hear the one about the bees that went on strike?

Punch Line: They wanted more honey and shorter working flowers!

When you follow the setup with a **buildup**, you delay the punch line. So when the punch line finally arrives, it seems even funnier. "Shaggy-dog stories"—long jokes with very complex story lines— are good examples of a buildup at work.

Can you identify the setup, buildup, and punch line in Dr. B. Hill-Arius's All-Time Favorite Shaggy-Dog Story?

Sally Smith was busy making dinner when the phone rang.

An eerie voice on the other end said, "Sally.... The Viper is coming for you," then hung up. Sally figured it was a prank call and forgot all about it.

Until the next day.

When the phone rang, she looked at it suspiciously. She answered it nervously.

"Sally.... The Viper is coming for you...soon," the eerie voice said.

The next day, Sally starting shaking as soon as the phone rang.

"Sally.... The Viper is coming for you...tomorrow!" said the eerie voice.

Sally didn't know what to do. She was so scared! She couldn't sleep that night. The next morning she couldn't eat her breakfast. She was pushing the cereal flakes around in her bowl...when the doorbell rang.

As if drawn by an invisible force, Sally crossed the hallway. She slowly opened the door. Right then, there was a clap of thunder!

There, on the front step, was a tiny little man in overalls. He was holding a bucket in one hand and a squeegee in the other.

"Hello, Sally," the small man said. "I am the viper. I am here to vipe your vindows!"

WHAT'S your TYPE?

There may be just one basic structure for a joke, but it can be used to create all kinds of funny stuff. It seems like wherever you look there's something funny going on!

FARCE

The word farce is used to describe comedy routines that rely on the improbable, the ridiculous, and the absurd. Mistaken identity and embarrassing situations are common subjects of farce. For more on farce, see the chapter on clowns.

SITUATION COMEDY

This type of humor puts characters into unusual situations. How they react to the situation, and to each other, is what delivers the laughs. In everyday speech, the term "situation comedy" has been shortened to "sitcom."

SIGHT GAGS

Sight gags are jokes that are visual. There are no words at all, just action. This action can be in a clown act, a comic strip, a movie, or a stand-up comedian's act. A clown whose tie curls up every time he tips his hat is performing a sight gag.

PARODY

A parody makes fun of something familiar by changing it so that what was once serious becomes silly. "Mary Had a Little Lamb" has been parodied more often than any other children's poem. Here's one:

Mary had a little lamb
You've heard it oft before
And then she passed her plate again
And had a little more

RIDDLES

Lots of people enjoy riddles. What makes them funny is when the solution involves an unexpected twist. Do you recognize these types of riddles?

The old "What's the difference...?" joke:

What's the difference between a giggling grizzly and an amusement park for rabbits?

One's a funny bear and the other's a bunny fair.

The question and answer joke:

What always ends everything?

The letter "g!"

The daffy definition:

Sales:

When people go buy-buy.

The good news/bad news gag:

The good news is that I made a huge batch of cookies! The bad news is that a horrible, hairy monster came to the door, demanded a snack, and gobbled them all up. And by the way, he's still hungry, and he's standing right behind you!

The cross-breed joke:

What do you get when you cross a dog with a hen?

Pooched eggs.

PUNS

Puns play with words that sound alike or have more than one meaning. Puns are sometimes called "groaners." People who say that are clearly no pun at a party.

What's the witch's favorite computer program?

The spell checker.

SLAPSTICK HUMOR

Slapstick humor is goofy and physical. When someone steps on a banana peel, trips over the dog, or gets a pie in the face—that's slapstick. The term originated with noisy props used in Ancient Greek comedies to make the sound of smacking.

MAKE YOUR OWN SLAPSTICK MITTS

These great mitts make an extra-loud smacking noise when clapped together. Like the Ancient Greek props, they add excitement and humor whenever a little clowning around is in order.

YOU'LL NEED

pencil and paper

ruler

scissors

135 cm (1½ yds.) vinyl fabric (available from a fabric store)

black marker

hole punch

2 large pieces of cardboard

stapler with staples

2 long shoelaces

pad of sticky note paper

① Using the picture (right) as a model, draw a mitten shape on a piece of paper. It should measure about 30 cm (12 in.) long and 15 cm (6 in.) wide. Cut out.

② Lay the vinyl fabric, shiny side down, on a table. Place the paper mitten cut-out on the vinyl with the thumb facing right. Using your marker, trace around the template.

③ Move the paper mitten to another spot on the vinyl and repeat step 2.

④ Now turn over the paper mitt so the thumb is pointing left. Lay it on the vinyl and trace it twice that way.

⑤ Cut out the four vinyl mitten shapes. Turn all four pieces shiny side up. Take one piece with the thumb on the left and one with the thumb on the right. These will be the **TOPS** of your mitts. Put the other two pieces aside.

⑥ Cut out a triangle from the bottom center of each **TOP** piece (where your wrist

18

will be). Each side of the triangle should be 5–7.5 cm (2–3 in.) long. Using the hole punch, punch a row of four holes on either side of the triangle—eight altogether for each mitt **TOP**. The holes should be about 1.5 cm ($\frac{1}{2}$ in.) apart.

⑦ Cut two rectangular pieces of cardboard that are narrower and slightly shorter than the body of the mitt— approximately 29 cm (11$\frac{1}{2}$ in.) long. These will help to stiffen your mittens and make the slapping sound.

⑧ Take the two remaining mitten pieces (the **BOTTOMS**) and flip them so they're shiny side down.

⑨ Place one piece of cardboard on top of each. Then place the **TOP** mitten pieces, shiny side up, on top of the cardboard to make a sandwich, lining up the thumbs on the **TOP** and **BOTTOM** pieces with the cardboard snugly fit inside its two covers.

⑩ Using your stapler, start at one edge of the wrist, and staple around the outside edge of vinyl to seal. **Do not close up the wrist!** Repeat with second mitt.

⑪ Insert one shoelace through the top two holes of one mitt. Lace like you are tying a shoe. Repeat for the second mitt.

⑫ Slip your hands into the mitts so that the cardboard rests against your palms.

⑬ Have someone tie the laces on your gloves so they don't fall off. Clap your mitts together. *Ta-dah!* Slapsticks!

Laff-Riot Recipes

DIRT CUPS

You'll Need

500 mL (2 cups) cold milk

1 package instant chocolate pudding mix (136 g./4.5 oz)

250 mL (8 oz.) tub frozen whipped topping

450 g (16 oz.) package chocolate wafers, crushed

8–10 small (10 cm/4 in.), clean plastic planter pots, lined with aluminum foil to cover holes in the base.

Serve with Tasty Earthworms (see right) or plain old gummi worms for an extra delicious treat!

You'll Also Need

measuring cups and spoons
mixing bowl • stirring spoon

1 Pour the milk into the mixing bowl. Add pudding mix. Stir and let stand for five minutes.

2 Stir in the frozen dessert topping and half of the wafer crumbs.

3 Place 15 mL (1 tbsp.) of wafer crumbs in each pot. Fill cups ¾ full with the pudding mixture.

4 Top the pudding in each pot with the remaining wafer crumbs. Decorate with worms.

Now food should be funny, don't you think? Play with these recipes (and look for others throughout the book) for fun in the kitchen and at the table.

TASTY EARTHWORMS

You'll Need

250 mL (1 cup) chocolate sprinkles or shredded coconut (or both)

60 mL (¼ cup) butter or margarine

60 mL (¼ cup) smooth peanut butter*

125 mL (½ cup) liquid honey

5 mL (1 tsp.) vanilla extract

375 mL (1½ cups) quick-cooking oats

80 mL (⅓ cup) dry milk powder

125 mL (½ cup) toasted wheat germ

30 mL (2 tbsp.) unsweetened cocoa powder

You'll Also Need

measuring cups and spoons
small, shallow bowl or pie plate
medium saucepan
wooden spoon • mixing bowl
waxed paper • cookie sheet

***ALLERGY ALERT:** If you are allergic to peanuts, substitute 60 mL (¼ cup) marshmallows for the peanut butter.*

1. Pour sprinkles and/or coconut into the bowl or pie plate and set aside. If you prefer to make worms in two different colors, use two bowls and keep the sprinkles and coconut separate.

2. In a medium saucepan over low heat, melt the butter with the peanut butter. You should ask an adult for help with this step. Stir the mixture until it is smooth and slimy—about 7 minutes.

3. Turn off stove element and remove the pan from heat. Stir in honey and vanilla.

4. In a separate bowl, mix together oats, milk powder, wheat germ, and cocoa. Dump the mixture into the peanut butter slime all at once. Stir quickly to mix. Be fast or the solids will clump. Allow mixture to cool until it is just warm to the touch—about 10 minutes.

5. Wash your hands. Using your fingers, grab a bit of the worm slop and roll it into wormoid shapes between your palms.

6. Then roll these worms in the chocolate sprinkles or coconut. Place finished worms on cookie sheet lined with waxed paper. Refrigerate until firm. Eat 'em up! Yum!

YIELD: makes about 24 worms

PREP. TIME: 30 minutes

How FUNNY Are You?

Well you know you can make your little brother laugh, but do you have what it takes to keep an audience rolling in the aisles? Take this quiz to find out! Record your answers on a separate piece of paper. When you are finished, add up your score using the chart at right. Are you a SCHOLAR OF SILLINESS, a GIGGLE-MASTER, or something in between?

1 Which word or phrase from Column B is best to finish each sentence from A?

Column A

1. My room is so small that the mice have ●———●.

2. What toys do T-rexes play with? ●———●

3. What do skeletons do before the big test? ●———●

4. What do frogs wear on St. Patrick's Day? ●———●

5. What does King Kong eat when he goes to a restaurant? ●———●

Column B

a. the restaurant

b. nothing

c. bone up

d. moved out

e. tricera-tops

O-1O
SCHOLAR OF SILLINESS
Seriously, now! Your sense of humor is subtle, and often unappreciated by others. Consider a career as an accountant.

2 Which is the funniest place name?

a) Moose Factory
b) Flin Flon
c) Detroit

3 Which animal is the funniest?

a) A duck-billed platypus in a beauty contest.
b) A three-toed sloth in the Indy 500.
c) Your dog.

4 Which would be the best birthday gift for your 98-year-old aunt?

a) A Whoopee cushion.
b) A unicycle.
c) Peace and quiet.

5 Which is the funniest food?

a) An apple.
b) Jiggling jelly.
c) "Poached Eggs" with "Bacon" (see page 108).

6 How do you know the elephants want to go swimming?

a) They look sweaty.
b) They are wearing trunks.
c) They have just thrown inflatable toys into the waterhole.

SCORING

For question 1, give yourself 1 point for each correct answer:

1–d, 2–e, 3–c, 4–b, 5–a

For questions 2 through 6, give yourself the following points:

2	a: 3	b: 5	c: 2
3	a: 3	b: 5	c: 2
4	a: 5	b: 2	c: 3
5	a: 2	b: 3	c: 5
6	a: 2	b: 3	c: 5

Add up your total and check against the laff-o-meter for your score.

10-15
HUMOROLOGIST
Let's talk! You prefer a good laugh to practicing your multiplication tables. You don't always get the joke, but that doesn't stop you from laughing. Enjoy yourself!

16-21
DR. LAFFAMINIT
You're the laff of the party. Wherever you go, you bring laughter with you. Of course, it might also be a good idea to bring a little giftie for the host, if you want to be invited back.

22-30
GIGGLE-MASTER
You funmeister! Your unerring wit and incredible sense of comic timing are so....ha-ha-ha... tee-hee...snort...! STOP!

Laff-o-Meter

Maggoty Mush

Opening Your Act

Stand-Up Comedy

Perfect Props

Improvisation

Don't Sit Down!

IS THIS THING ON?

Tap! Tap!

Think you might like to be a comedian? Then you've come to the right place. This handy-dandy guide to stand-up comedy will get you started.

Tips from the Pros

Stand-up comics don't just get up on stage and tell jokes. They actually prepare for years to get their routines right! Practice is important—telling jokes to a room full of strangers is very different from yukking it up with your friends in the cafeteria. Read on to learn more secrets of the pros.

TELLING TIMING

You already know the basics of a joke: setup, buildup, punch line. But *how you tell* that joke makes all the difference between blowing away the audience and bombing big time. The key is timing. Some people have it naturally; others need to work harder at it— but all comedians need to practice it.

• First, speak loudly and clearly, and not too fast. This might seem simple, but it's where most beginners fumble. If you mumble your jokes, the audience will not respond to your punch lines.

• Second, be a little "spacey." Many comedians take an extra beat—a silence—just before or after they deliver the punch line. Add a funny gesture, and the audience might just be howling.

Practice your timing by telling the same joke a few times, but varying the timing. How do you know when you've got your timing right? It's simple: people laugh.

Doing a Double-Take

A beat is such a wonderful thing, it can even be taken twice in a row! It's called a double-take. You take a beat, maybe by looking at the audience or something offstage. Look like you are about to continue on with your act, then take another beat. Done properly, a double-take can deliver double laughs.

ASK ME WHAT'S WRONG WITH KARL'S JOKES.

OK, I'LL BITE. WHAT'S WRONG WITH—

—TIMING!

B♀DY Lingo

Sometimes, the way a comic moves on the stage is funny enough on its own to get the audience laughing. Some famous comedians use a very silly walk, others wave their arms a lot or fidget nervously on stage. Ready to perfect your own body language for mega-laughs?

> MY OWN MOTHER FORGOT TO PICK ME UP AT THE AIRPORT!

> MY OWN MOTHER FORGOT TO PICK ME UP AT THE AIRPORT!

ONE JOKE SERVED TWO WAYS

See how body language makes all the difference to how the exact same line comes across? When you tell a joke, the expression on your face, your posture, or the way you gesture with your hands provide humor right along with your words.

Are you enthusiastic, or more subdued? Are there gestures you use a lot when you talk? Exaggerate your own personal style, then use it in your act.

28

Be Careful or Your Face Will STICK Like That

You already know the simple beauty of making a really great goofy face. If just crossing your eyes can draw a laugh, think of what you can do with a well-timed stare, wince, raised eyebrow, or grimace.

Experiment making faces in a mirror. Can your face show anger, fear, bewilderment, or other emotions in a comical way? What can you make your face say by twitching your eyebrow, furrowing your brow, biting your lip, or rolling your eyes? When the mirror laughs, you've got it down!

PULLING A FACE

Grinning and face-making contests used to be popular events hundreds of years ago in Britain. Today, a form of these grinning contests still exists in Cumbria, England. The contestants are always people who have no teeth. They can make incredible faces by thrusting their jaws forward and over the front of their faces, sometimes even sucking their noses into their mouths!

DEADPAN DAN

Some comedians use very controlled expressions—they may even look bored, miserable, or serious. It's a style called deadpan. A deadpan comic could say "My dog woke up this morning, jumped on the exercise bike, and started singing in Swedish" in the flattest of tones. The audience laughs because the comic's outlandish words are at odds with the ho-hum delivery.

Shtick 'Em Up!

PEOPLE SAY I'M TOO HYPER....

So you've got good timing, and great body language. But maybe you need something more...something to let your audience know that You Are Unique. What you need is a shtick—a gimmick, gag, or funny outfit—that is yours and yours alone.

WHERE SHTICK COMES FROM

The word shtick comes from a Yiddish word meaning "a little piece." It was originally used to refer to a small part in a play. Today, it refers to the bits of a comic's act that give it its special flavor.

PICK YOUR SHTICK

Your shtick might be a comic stage personality: a worrier, a klutz, or a know-it-all, for instance. Shtick can also be a comic appearance. Perhaps you wear a tuxedo, clothes that are too big or too small, a pair of funky glasses, mismatched clothes, or a kooky hairstyle.

Maybe you are really good at doing impressions of others, or you can mimic the sound of a plane or do other crazy sound effects. Perhaps your talent is making up silly songs, speaking in a weird accent, or multiplying big numbers in your head. Whatever your special talent, turn it into your shtick for a fabulous, one-of-a-kind performance.

COINING A CATCHPHRASE

One of the best forms of shtick is the catchphrase—a line you repeat throughout your act. It defines your comic personality, and it's a signal for your audience so people know when to laugh.

To create a catchphrase, first decide what your comic personality is. Are you a downtrodden student with too much homework and not enough time for fun? Maybe your catchphrase is: "I'VE GOT SO MUCH HOMEWORK!"

As you create your routine, use your catchphrase to tie different parts of your act together. Say it in an exaggerated or unusual way so that it will stick in your audience's heads.

Perfect PROPS

Sometimes, your shtick will come in the form of an object. The object is your prop—it "props" up your act and gives a focus to your routine. What makes a good prop? A prop can be absolutely anything: a horn, a telephone, a violin. Think of some famous comedians. What kinds of props do they use?

When choosing a prop, keep in mind that some objects are naturally funny. Stilts and cows are naturally funny (but hard to carry around). Textbooks and watches are not. Some funny objects are "interactive"—they allow your audience to get in on the act. Hand buzzers and squirting flowers are examples of funny interactive props. Consider adding one to your act.

Check out the list of funny objects below. Try working them, or any other favorites of your own, into your routine as a prop.

accordion	eggbeater	baby bottle
rubber duck	fake flower	beach ball
ball of wool	funny wig	snowshoes
stuffed fish	headphones	top hat
shower cap and bath brush	umbrella	bicycle horn

TRUNK O' LAFFS

Getting Your Act

Y ou've figured out your comic personality and developed your look. You've perfected your timing and your body language so that even your pet guppy laughs itself sick when you raise your left eyebrow. You've even decided on a catchphrase or a prop. How do you turn all of these bits and pieces into a full-fledged stand-up routine?

CHOOSING YOUR SUBJECT

When you are coming up with your routine, think carefully about the topics you will include. Talk about subjects everyone knows or types of personalities everyone is familiar with: the nervous Nellie, the rude party guest, the class bully. If your audience can recognize people or situations, or— even better—if they recognize themselves, you're more likely to get laughs.

THE MONOLOGUE

A monologue is a spoken performance with only one actor: you. It shouldn't be just a string of unconnected jokes. The gags need to be connected together to form a seamless whole. Your monologue should include:

☆ an opener: to introduce yourself to your audience when you first come on stage

☆ a bit: your first grouping of connected jokes

☆ a transition: a way to lead you from your first bit to your second bit; sometimes called a segue (pronounced SEG-way)

☆ another bit

☆ another transition

☆ a closing

OPENER

BIT

T-o-g-e-t-h-e-r

UP-TO-THE-MINUTE LAUGHS

Experts say that each minute of your routine should have four jokes, or two jokes and one funny story. A good guideline is that you should make the audience laugh at least once every 15 seconds.

To start out, put together a three-minute routine. Make sure your routine includes at least one really funny minute. Your audience will remember that you were funny, at least part of the time. Read on for great tips for a killer routine over the next few pages.

Start Off Strong

Start your act with your funniest stuff to get your audience laughing right away. If you save your best bits for the end, you may have lost your audience's interest. But if you open with your funniest stuff, and you get your audience laughing, they will be more likely to laugh at even your less side-splitting bits.

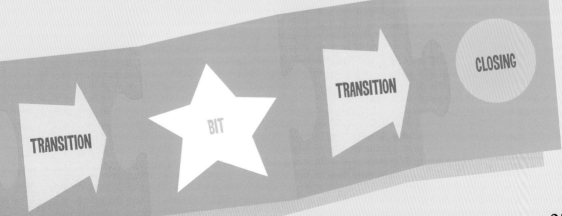

TRANSITION

BIT

TRANSITION

CLOSING

Opening your Act

First things first: you need to get your audience's attention. A good way to do this is to start with an opener that draws them in. Your first words should also establish your character. So if, for example, your shtick is that you are a student with too much homework, you might start by saying:

> "THANKS SO MUCH! I'M SO GLAD TO BE HERE. YOU KNOW, I ALMOST DIDN'T MAKE IT BECAUSE *I'VE GOT SO MUCH HOMEWORK!*"

Then dive right into your first joke. Make it a good one. Make it short.

Don'ts

Don't start your routine by saying, "Here's a joke for you, it's really funny."

Don't start with, "Did you hear the one about...."

Don't say, "Stop me if you've heard this one before."

Don't say, "Do you want to hear a joke?"

DON'T STEP ON YOUR LAUGH

Ahhh…it's music to your ears! They are laughing! Whatever you do, don't start your next line until the laughter dies down. If you do, the audience will miss the beginning of your next joke. They'll also resent you for interrupting their giggles. And it'll be harder to make them laugh the next time. So leave lots of time for those oh-so precious laughs.

Milking a Gag

The opposite of stepping on your laugh is "milking a gag." Comedians do this in different ways: by pausing, repeating, or making a face to get the biggest and longest laugh out of each joke. Milking a gag is a fine art, and not easy to do. An old proverb says: "Milk the cow, but don't pull off the udders!"

WHAT IF THEY'RE NOT LAUGHING?

Again, don't rush. Zipping on to your next joke makes you seem nervous and insecure. The audience will smell blood, and will turn on you. Instead, stay confident and relaxed. Just because they are not laughing out loud doesn't mean they are not laughing inside, right? Of course you're funny! So keep your cool and your timing. And remember not to laugh at your own jokes! Leave that to your audience.

ON TO YOUR FIRST BIT

Your first bit is the next step. You can put together a bunch of unrelated jokes, but they won't work too well unless you figure out how to pull them together. So link them with a common theme. If the opening is about school, stay there for a while. Don't stick in a joke about your grandmother's birthday present next.

Choosing your Words

Y ou've collected some jokes for your first bit, a bit you are calling "Bowlerama." How can you make them even funnier? In any routine, just as in every "What I Did on My Summer Vacation" essay, your choice of words makes the difference between an A+ and a detention.

First, write out the joke on a piece of paper: "My friend George likes to go bowling. The last time he went, though, the bowling alley was on strike." Read the joke. Laugh. Now ask yourself, how can I make this joke even funnier?

Reword the joke to take out any unnecessary or repeated words. Look for ways to make the remaining words more colorful. For example, take out "to go." Replace "bowling alley" with "pins."

Exaggerate. Does George like to bowl, or love to bowl? Maybe he is crazy about bowling. Does he bowl at the bowling alley or at the Sunset Bowlerama? Does he specialize in gutter balls?

Then, listen to the sound of the words. Some words—like parsnip, spatula, nostril, or frizzled—simply sound funnier than others. Try adding words that strike you as hilarious to your routine.

REPHRASE IT

Now that you've replaced any dull words, see if you can make your joke sound like something you might say in conversation. Your joke may now go like this: "My friend George is addicted to bowling. The other day, he hurried off to the Sunset Bowlerama for his daily game. (I wanted to go too, but I couldn't because I HAD SO MUCH HOMEWORK!) It turned out he couldn't play because the pins were on strike."

Reread your joke. Is the meaning clear? Does the surprise come at the end? Is the punch line punchy? If you answered yes, give yourself a pat on the back, and move on to your second joke. Make sure it links to the theme of your first joke. For example, "The bowling balls had no sympathy for the pins. They just kept yelling, 'Oh, spare me!'" Try your jokes out together. Follow up with one more gag on the same theme, like: "And you know those funky shoes you to have to wear to bowl? They were fit to be tied."

Practice your three jokes together. Where should you take extra beats? Where should you use a funny gesture or make a face? Practice until you can recite the whole bit all together and get a laugh—or three—every time. Congratulations! You have crafted your first comic bit.

GET CREATIVE

If you can't think of a funny word, go ahead and make one up. Lewis Carroll, the author of *Alice in Wonderland*, created dozens of funny words, including "chortle" (a combination of snort and chuckle) and "Jabberwocky."

The gorilla in the zoo was expecting a baby. When the happy event occurred, the zookeeper put up a sign on the front gates: "It's a girlilla!"

Blockbusting Moves

Do you have gag-writer's block? Try these tips to jump-start your funny.

- Write three one-liners about: food, the weather, family vacations.

- Write a one-minute long story about: something that happened to you in second grade; a trip to the zoo; yo-yos; a grilled-cheese sandwich.

- Work on an impression of: a celebrity, someone at school, your aunt, your mom's best friend, a baby, a cat with a furball.

- Describe the plot of a recent movie without using any nouns other than the word "thing."

- Keep a joke journal. Write down ideas that seem funny to you. Refer to your journal when writing new gags for a routine.

- Leaf through a joke book. Find a joke you like. Rewrite it to make it fresh and original.

- Finish these sentences: "My dog is so smart, he…" "My piano teacher is so crazy, she…" "My nose is so sensitive, it…"

- Look at pictures in a magazine or newspaper. Imagine funny captions for them.

WORKING WITH ANOTHER COMIC

If getting up on stage alone seems intimidating, you're right. It's tough to go it alone. Having a partner means that you share the work, and you double the chances that the audience will like you!

If you think you'd like to be part of a comic team, here are some things you should know:

- Most comedy duos have one partner who provides the straight lines (so is called the straight man or straight woman).

- The straight player feeds the lines to the gag player. The gag player gets the first laugh, by making all the jokes, doing all the pratfalls, and creating all the comic situations.

- The straight player then gets his or her turn, by reacting to the gag player. Whether the reaction is shock or anger, dismay or disappointment, the straight player will get the second laugh, and the sympathy of the audience.

When you decide to work with a partner, choose which one of you will be the straight player and which will be the gag player. In general, you should stick to these roles for your entire act. (For more on working with a partner, see chapter 3 on clowns.)

Moving Right Along

You began your monologue with a bit about bowling. Your second bit might be about your classmate Wilma. Wilma is crazy about movies. She keeps asking you to go to the movies with her, but you can never go, because…

YOU'VE GOT SO MUCH HOMEWORK!
(Remember your catchphrase!)

How do you get from your jokes about George to your gags about Wilma? You need a transition—a bridge between bits. A good transition might go something like this: **"My friend Wilma almost laughed herself sick the day George came to class wearing a vintage bowling shirt, and looking like something out of an old movie. You see, Wilma's crazy about movies…"**

WRAPPING IT UP

A good monologue, like any good story, needs a solid ending, or closing. It should tie up any loose ends, and somehow bring the story back to the beginning. Say, for example, you continue your monologue with a third hilarious bit about learning to ski. You've been talking long enough, your throat is dry, and it's time to wrap it up.

Your closing could go something like this: **"Yeah, learning to ski was quite a challenge. Of course I'd be better if I could spend more time at it but who has time when you HAVE SO MUCH HOMEWORK?! I tell you, I'm about ready to go on strike myself. The problem is, I'd have to deal with George pulling me to my feet and shouting 'Reset! Reset!'"**

Your audience will laugh because they remember George, and now they are in on the joke. They'll laugh because you brought your act full circle. And they'll laugh because you used your catchphrase again in yet another funny way.

LEAVE 'EM LAUGHING

Vaudeville shows, popular a hundred years ago, featured comic skits, songs, dancing, and acrobatics. They remained extremely popular until "moving picture shows" came along in the 1920s. The old vaudeville rule "Always leave 'em laughing" is still a good one.

Make sure to close with a surefire joke, a great big thank you to the audience, and a compliment of how great they were. Take a bow, and gracefully leave the stage.

TROUBLESHOOTING

...YOU FORGET WHAT YOU WERE GOING TO SAY NEXT

Everybody blanks now and then. Just skip what you had planned to say. Don't try to go back and reconstruct it. If you are really floundering, stick in a prepared line as a stop gap before moving on to your next bit. Something like: "Gosh, I can barely think straight, because I HAVE SO MUCH HOMEWORK!"

...NOBODY LAUGHS AT ONE OF YOUR BEST JOKES

Fuggedaboudit. Go on to the next gag, behaving exactly as if they had laughed. They're laughing inside, right?

POP!

...SOMEONE HECKLES YOU

Stand-up comedy is hard enough without having to compete with someone in the audience. The best approach to hecklers is to ignore them. If they really get in your face, though, you will have to deal with them. Don't worry, the audience will be on your side.

The Magical Heckler-Deflator

Is there a bag of wind in the audience who's giving you trouble? Here are some comebacks for bursting his or her bubble.

• Oh, what do we have here? And my obnoxious detector wasn't even blinking!

• Ladies and gentlemen: the Personality Transplant "before" picture.

• See what happens when you don't eat a nutritious breakfast?

• And for his next trick, he claps his hands!

• I'm sorry, your prize was not your own comedy show. Please go to the nearest exit immediately and report to the nice lady holding the straitjacket.

• Is there a doctor in the house?

• Ladies and gentlemen—in case you were wondering why I am so odd, I'd like you to meet my mother. Isn't she just so lovely? Thanks, Mom, for everything.

• Thank you, sir, your feedback is appreciated. Would you care to write it down? (As you're saying this, hand over a tiny notepad with a huge, oversized pencil.)

A Word about BOMBING

Everybody bombs—even the greats. Performing a routine where nobody laughs is a rite of passage in the world of stand-up comedy. And since practicing in front of an audience is the only way to improve, you will inevitably bomb a lot at the beginning of your career. Follow these tips from the pros to reduce the number of your bombs.

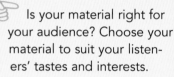 Is your material right for your audience? Choose your material to suit your listeners' tastes and interests.

Pay attention to the world around you. Read the newspaper. Watch people in the street. Remember that your best routine will be true to your own personality, style, and "take" on the world. No one but you sees things the way you do.

After every routine, note where the audience did not laugh. Ask yourself what went wrong. Was your delivery flat? Was your timing off? Was the joke dumb? Did they just not hear it?

Is your material offensive? Jokes about ethnic groups or other minorities are not funny. Dirty words or bathroom humor are not funny. Topics such as death do not make for successful acts either. Eliminate these from your routine.

Vary your pacing. Add in some longer stories, or some one-liners. Make sure every joke doesn't follow the same formula.

Listen to and learn from the pros. How would your favorite comedian handle this material?

Practice in front of a mirror. Do you look relaxed and comfortable? If you are uncomfortable, your audience will be tense too, and not likely to laugh.

How big was your audience? Professional comedians know that the larger the crowd, the easier it is to get a laugh. Scary though it may be, try to play to a bigger audience next time.

What kind of mood was your audience in? An audience full of people who know each other will be more receptive than one full of strangers.

Eliminate any jokes that don't get laughs in two or more performances.

LAUGHTER—PASS IT ON

Comedians know that laughter is contagious. Get one good belly-laugher in the audience, and the whole crowd will follow suit. That's why TV producers add laugh tracks to sitcoms. It's also why, when you see a funny movie in the theater with a large, enthusiastic audience, you're probably more likely to laugh out loud than if you watch it at home, alone, on a DVD.

Laff-Riot Recipes II

MAGGOTY MUSH

You'll Need

125 mL (½ cup) short-grain rice, uncooked

1 L (4 cups) milk

80 mL (⅓ cup) sugar

5 mL (1 tsp.) vanilla extract

60 mL (¼ cup) raisins

cinnamon to taste

You'll Also Need

measuring cup and spoons

large, microwave-safe mixing bowl

wooden spoon

plastic wrap • fork

It looks so nasty, but tastes so nice!

1. In a large, microwave-safe bowl, combine the rice, milk, and sugar. Stir with the wooden spoon to combine.

2. Cover tightly with plastic wrap. Poke some holes in the wrap with a fork to allow steam to escape. Microwave on high for 8 to 10 minutes, until it comes to a boil. Ask a grownup for help with steps using the microwave.

3. Remove plastic wrap. Be careful! Wear oven mitts if the bowl is hot. The steam that can escape is very, very hot!

4. Stir with the wooden spoon, and then return the bowl to the microwave. Leave it uncovered. Cook on medium (50 percent power) for 40 to 45 minutes. Stop and stir every 10 minutes. The mush is done when the rice (the "maggots") is soft and the mush is creamy.

5. Remove from the microwave. Using the fork, gently stir in vanilla and raisins. Sprinkle top with cinnamon. Serve warm with more milk poured over top, or chilled.

YIELD: makes 4 servings

PREP. TIME: 1 hour

Did your routine not go off as well as you'd hoped? Don't mope! Try one of these culinary treats instead. The results are guaranteed. No one could still feel glum after chewing on a goblin eyeball...right?

GHOULISH GOBLIN EYEBALLS

You'll Need

One 230 g (8 oz.) can whole pitted lychees in syrup (available in large supermarkets in the canned fruits section)

blueberries

green food dye

You'll Also Need

can opener • mixing spoon

slotted spoon • serving platter

YIELD: about 20 eyeballs

PREP. TIME: 30 minutes

"Goblin eyeballs for dinner — again?!!"

1. Open can of lychees.
2. Drop 30 drops of green food coloring into the can. Stir well. Allow the mixture to sit for a few minutes until the lychees absorb some of the dye and turn a ghastly shade of green.
3. If the lychees are not evenly colored, add a bit more dye and stir again.
4. Using the slotted spoon, remove the lychees from the can. Reserve the syrup if you want to serve the goblin eyes in their own gunk.
5. Carefully insert one blueberry into the hole in each lychee (where the "nut" once was) to make the eyeball.
6. Arrange finished eyeballs on a serving platter.

Improvisation

Many comedians get their training as part of an improv team—a group of actors who create skits that are improvised, or created on the spot without scripts. The actors have to work together and use their imaginations to craft a funny scene in front of the audience!

Squeeze-a-Snake

Doing improv keeps you on your toes. This silly serpent game helps you build your speed, focus, and memory.

YOU'LL NEED

4 or more players

1 Arrange yourselves in a circle, holding hands.

2 One player starts the game by squeezing the hand of the player either to the left or right.

3 The person whose hand is squeezed must quickly squeeze the hand of the next person in the circle. The squeeze will pass around, like a "wave" in a stadium. Players should not communicate, through words or gestures, when they have been squeezed.

4 Once the first squeeze is traveling around the circle, any player can add another squeeze at any time. The new squeeze can be longer or shorter than the first, or be a double- or triple-squeeze made up of two or three short pulses. Players will have to pay attention to not get mixed up!

INSTANT FUN!

Members of improv teams need to find out about each other's strengths. To train, improv players do special exercises that help them develop their humorous imaginations. Try these traditional improv activities as a way to develop your own comic skills, or just to have fun with your friends.

Pleased to Meet Ya!

In this game, you'll learn how to stay in character while responding to the different cues you get from your improv teammates.

YOU'LL NEED

4 or more players

1 game guide

1 Each player should think of a character that they are going to be for the game—a rock star, a pirate, a kid bouncing a ball, etc.—but keep it to themselves.

2 When the game guide shouts "Start!" all the players walk around the room, acting in character.

3 When the guide says "Stop!" the players say hello and greet their closest neighbor, in character, like *a long, lost friend*.

4 The game guide quickly shouts "Go!" and the players resume wandering around the room.

5 Next time the game guide shouts "Stop!" the players greet the nearest person like *an enemy*.

6 As the game continues, the game guide should direct players with a new way to greet each other each time. Players can switch roles so that the guide can play too.

7 After you have finished playing, have players guess what character each person was playing.

Mirror, Mirror on the Wall

Are you in synch with your improv partner? Try this "reflective" game to see.

YOU'LL NEED

2 or more players

1. Team up into pairs of two.

2. Team members should face each other. Hold up your hands in front as if you are touching an invisible mirror between you.

3. Without touching each other, partners should "mirror" each other's movements. There is no leader and no follower—either player can move as desired. The trick is to keep all the movements synchronized! Slow, gradual gestures are easier to mimic than fast, jerky ones.

4. Don't forget to change partners for variety!

more Improv

WE'RE COMPLETELY IN SYNCH!

Very Silly Walk-a-thon

To be a good physical comedian, you have to free up your body to move in unusual and funny ways. Get ready to get silly!

YOU'LL NEED

a group of friends

1. Have players begin walking around the room normally.

2. One player shouts out the name of a body part. Players must pretend that that body part is leading them around the room. For example, if "elbow" is called out, imagine a puppeteer's string is yanking your elbow in a series of jerks, or in one smooth motion. How fast is up to you—just make sure your elbow always leads. (Watch out for other players' noggins!)

3. What else could make this walk funny? Maybe you try to ignore or resist the pull? Maybe you're embarrassed and try to hide it? Maybe you get angry?

4. Continue until someone shouts out a new body part, then change.

Happy Birthday Box

This game, for three or more players, gives you practice in exaggerating your reactions. Begin with the first player pretending to open a box. He or she should react to what's in the box—with surprise, joy, horror, whatever. Player one then pretends to close the box and hands it to the next player. The second player opens the box, and reacts in the same way as the first, but exaggerates the reaction. Continue exaggerating each reaction until the last player performs a completely over-the-top version of the initial reaction. Repeat, changing the order in which players go, and the reaction.

even more Improv

Freeze-Frame Presentation

In improv, players act out a story "on the fly." They don't know where the story is going! Try this out in a fun way with friends.

1. Assemble the group into pairs. Each pair will tell a story to the audience.

2. Within the pair, decide who is the storyteller, and who will act it out.

3. The actor acts out the story like "slides" in a slide-show. So, for example, the narrator begins the story: "Madison was walking through the woods...." He claps to display a "slide," and the second player freezes in a position that illustrates that part of the story.

4. The narrator continues the story, "clapping" several times to show "slides" for the story.

5. Keep switching places to allow another team to tell and show a story, and to let everyone have a turn as both an actor and a storyteller.

"Once Upon a Time" Storytelling

Create an improv piece of your own!

YOU'LL NEED

a group of friends

two fish bowls
(or other bowls or hats)

paper • pen • scissors

1 Cut a sheet (or two) of paper into small pieces. Have players write the names of ordinary objects—for example, puzzle, wig, apple, dog, etc.—on half of the pieces of paper.

2 On the remaining pieces of paper, have players write action words—such as climb, dance, capture, twist, etc. Make lots of them! The more you have, the better the game will be.

3 Fold each slip of paper. Put the object slips in one bowl and the action slips in another.

4 One player chooses a slip of paper from each bowl, then reads out what's on them to the group. The mission, now, is to create a fairytale skit that uses these two words. For example, if the player selected "climb" and "wig," you might decide to act out a version of Jack and the Beanstalk where the giant has lost a wig. You won't know where the story will go, because you discuss only the basic idea with your partners, then you just dive right in.

5 The person who selected the two slips of paper begins the skit by acting and talking in the role of a character. For example, the player might begin as Jack planting the magic beans.

6 The next player who has an idea to move the story along jumps into the scene as another character. For example, the next player might enter the scene as the cow.

7 All the players should jump in and out of the scene until the story comes to a funny yet satisfying conclusion.

Story Circle

In this simple but hilarious exercise, you'll need at least two friends to build a funny story together. Begin by having a player start a story by reciting the first line. For example, "Once upon a time there was a carnivorous hamster named Polly." The second player continues the story. "Polly was especially fond of jellied toes of girls named Sue." Continue the story, with each player adding a new line until it's done.

Clowning Around

Clown Fashion 101

How to Juggle

Clown Techniques

Makeup Magic

Clown Gags

DISCOVER THE CLOWN IN YOU

Is there a clown in you just bursting to get out? Where stand-up comedians use words to get most of their laughs, clowns usually use their actions. They dance, sing, fall on their faces, trip over invisible dogs, or bump into each other on the way through a door.

Most clowns rely on this kind of "physical comedy," but their acts can still be very different from each other. Look at the next page. Which list best describes the way you like to act when you are being funny? Look below the lists to find out what that says about what type of clown you might be.

Column A

clumsy

outgoing

goofy

forgetful

talkative/like to use sound effects

prefer bright, mismatched clothing

Column B

like to pretend to be a particular character, like a mad scientist or fairy princess

neither very loud nor very quiet

innocent

enjoy drawing others into a fantasy

like to sing, or speak in made-up voice

prefer a costume, such as a firefighter or knight

Column C

refined

reserved

sophisticated

stuck-up

silent/like to use facial expressions

prefer elegant, shimmery clothing

YOUR CLOWN TYPE

If **column B** describes you best, you might prefer to be a Character Clown. (See page 62.)

If **column C** describes you best, you might prefer to be a Pierrot Clown. (See page 61.)

If **column A** describes you best, you might be a perfect Auguste Clown. (See page 60.)

If **two or more lists** apply to you, you might be a natural Comedy Whiteface Clown. (See page 63.)

Read on to find out all about clowns!

59

Kinds of Clowns

The three main types of clowns are: the Auguste, the Pierrot, and the Character clown.

The Auguste

The Auguste is the red-nosed buffoon in baggy pants that we usually think of when we say "clown." Think bright, clashing colors, floppy shoes, patched clothing, garish makeup, and a kooky wig.

Auguste means "foolish" in German. Auguste clowns misunderstand basic instructions, foul things up, and get carried away. They are good-natured but clumsy— always tripping, falling, and accidentally whacking others with their props.

The Pierrot

The Pierrot is the opposite of the Auguste. Where the Auguste is clumsy, the Pierrot is elegant. Where the Auguste is foolish and ridiculous, the Pierrot is sophisticated and smart. The Pierrot's style lends itself well to the art of mime (acting without words).

Pierrots have a different look to match their style. They wear a simple costume, usually in one or two colors, in fabrics that gleam or shimmer. Their hats are plain cones—maybe with a turned-up brim. Face makeup is usually all white with just small details. A female Pierrot is sometimes called a Pierrette or a Pirouette.

THE PERFECT PAIR

When the Pierrot and the Auguste work together, the Pierrot is the straight player and the Auguste delivers the gag (see also page 41).

A typical Auguste-Pierrot routine might have the Pierrot trying to do a simple task, such as watering a flower. The Auguste tries to help, and in the process, knocks the Pierrot down, dirties his clothes, spills the water, soaks the Pierrot's shoes, knocks the Pierrot down again, and eventually kills the flower. The audience laughs *at* the Auguste's ridiculous antics, and sympathizes *with* the Pierrot. The more exasperated the Pierrot becomes, the funnier the act.

more
Kinds of Clowns

The Character Clown

The character clown is a real-life cartoon. The character can be any familiar type: a mad scientist, a delicate fairy, a cranky baby, or a demanding king, for example.

One type of character clown, the Tramp (or Hobo), became extremely popular during the first half of the 1900s. The Tramp has become so well known that it has turned into its own category. In a clown troupe, the Tramp will be the victim of all of the other clowns.

Weary Willie

Emmett Kelly, an American circus performer, created one of the most famous clown characters of all time, "Weary Willie." Weary Willie wore the shabby clothing of a Tramp, but he was different. Up until then, all clowns wore whiteface and performed slapstick stunts for laughs. But Willie was tragic, not comic. His most famous routine involved sweeping up the circus floor after other performers had finished their acts. He kept trying to sweep away a pool of light left by a single spotlight. The audience watched, and laughed and cried at the same time.

The Comedy Whiteface

The Comedy Whiteface clown blends different parts of different clown styles, such as a whiteface and baggy clothes, to create a unique character. The Comedy Whiteface clown is probably the most common kind of clown seen today.

Lassoing for Laughs

Rodeo clowns have one of the most dangerous jobs in all of show business. They protect other rodeo performers from bucking horses or charging bulls. Rodeo clowns wear oversized, loose-fitting, and brightly colored clothing to perform their stunts and to distract the animals, which allows the other performers to get to safety. They have to be expert horseback riders and have a great sense of humor. They also have to have a terrific sense of timing, keen wits, and lots of courage.

What Would You Do...?

Picture this: a girl hands you a bouquet of flowers. What would you do if you were...

...an Auguste?

You might clap your hands, jump up and down, then lean over the bouquet to take a big, noisy sniff of the flowers. Your nose would start to itch. You'd try to hold back a sneeze. You'd start...to ah, ah, ah-choo! And blow the flowers all over the room. You'd try to wipe the sneeze off the child and at the same time pick up the flowers, which of course keep falling to the ground.

...a Character Clown?

Are you a mad scientist? You might start examining them with a magnifying glass. A police officer? You might give the child a ticket. A cowboy? You might get out your lasso to try and wrangle the flowers.

...a Pierrot?

You might first look around to see if anyone is watching. You'd thank the child very formally. You'd reach for the flowers, then wonder what to do with them. You'd sniff them reluctantly. You'd ask the Auguste for a vase, who then drops the vase and tries to take the flowers from you at the same time. You'd get annoyed with the Auguste's bumbling.

...a Comedy Whiteface Clown?

You might gleefully take the flowers and toss them one by one into the air. You might use them to decorate your outfit. You might give them to someone else, or to the audience members.

64

MEET SOME FAMOUS EARLY CLOWNS

Albert Fratellini was one of the celebrated Fratellini Brothers who clowned in Europe in the first half of the twentieth century. He was the first clown to use a red nose in his act.

Lou Jacobs worked as a clown for the Ringling Bros. & Barnum and Bailey Circus for more than 60 years, starting in the 1920s. Jacobs, who invented the miniature clown car, is in the Clowning Hall of Fame.

Joseph Grimaldi was one of the greatest English clowns. He first appeared in 1805 and excelled in tumbling, pratfalls, and slapstick. In honor of Grimaldi, circus clowns began referring to themselves and each other as "Joeys," a term that is still used today.

Grock was the "king of the clowns" during the early twentieth century. One of his most famous routines involved playing a violin on which the strings suddenly disappeared! Of course, the audience could see that he was simply holding the instrument upside down.

Charlie Chaplin became a star in 1916 with his Tramp character. He appeared in several movies as the Tramp, including *The Kid*, *The Gold Rush*, and *Modern Times*.

SILENCE IS GOLDEN?

Decide ahead of time if you want to mime—work silently—or speak aloud during your routine. It's your choice. Great clown routines are performed both ways. Try to picture each of the flower routines at left first as done by a mime (maybe with sound effects?), and second, by a speaking clown (with a funny voice?). Which version appeals to you?

CLOWN FASHION 101

AUGUSTE ATTIRE

Make your hat extra large or extra small.

Choose clothes that are either way *too* big or way too small (or both). The pants have got to be baggy!

Choose bright, mismatched colors and patterns, like stripes, checks, flowers, or polka dots. Big patterns are best.

Suspenders and a bowtie or tie—zanier is better (wear on your bare neck for extra laffs).

Add secret pockets. You can hide your props or tricks inside them. (See page 86.)

Add patches. Sew them on with brightly colored yarn.

A big part of clowning is the clothing. Your look will have a huge impact on your audience. Check out some clown closets for fabulous fashion finds.

Striped, patterned, or mismatched socks.

A colorful, kooky wig.

Big gloves.

Don't forget the big shoes. See how to make them at right.

CLOWN SHOES

YOU'LL NEED

a pair of tennis shoes (your own)

a very large pair of adult shoes (canvas sneakers in a bright color work well) with mismatched laces

newspaper

1 Stuff the front end of the large shoes with balled-up newspaper.

2 Slip your own shoes inside the bigger shoes.

3 Add more paper to keep your own shoes from sliding around inside the larger ones.

4 Slip your feet into your own shoes and tie them up. Tie the larger shoes on top.

5 Practice walking around in the shoes. If you find you simply can't walk, switch to funny slippers or other odd footwear, like bowling shoes. Tripping and really hurting yourself isn't funny at all.

TIPS FROM THE PROS

Check out your look in a mirror. Stand far away, so you can see how your costume will look to an audience. Change any item that doesn't look great or that doesn't let you move easily.

PIERROT'S WARDROBE

Make your hat a simple cone, maybe with a turned-up brim. Look for one in a party supply store, or make your own (see right).

Wear your hair neatly tied back, or hide it completely by covering with the top of a pair of white tights, cut and knotted to form a skullcap.

Choose a one- or two-piece outfit in the same color in a shimmery fabric. Satin pajamas work well. Your clothes should not be too big or too small.

Wear tight-fitting white kneesocks or other socks to match your outfit.

Decorate your costume with sparkles, beads, pompoms, glitter, bows, or bells. Not too many decorations—just to add a touch of glamor and fun.

Wear tight-fitting white gloves.

Loop a glimmery scarf around your waist. Tie the ankles and wrists of your outfit with matching fabric.

A ruff for around your neck.

Use ballet slippers or other simple shoes.

PIERROT'S HAT

YOU'LL NEED

a large piece of bristol board
tape • pencil • scissors
ruler • elastic string • glue
decorations (pompoms, glitter, or
ribbon to match your outfit)

1 Roll the bristol board into a cone shape to fit on your head. Tape to hold shape.

2 Place the cone on your head. If it's too loose, use a pencil to lightly mark a line where the cone rests at your forehead. This is where you will cut the cone to fit.

3 Using your scissors, cut up to the pencil line, then cut a straight line all around the cone. Try the cone on your head again. Does it fit? Cut it a little shorter if it keeps slipping down over your forehead.

4 Cut a piece of elastic string about 15 cm (6 in.) long. With the point of the scissors, make a small hole in either side of your hat (keeping the seam at the back). Thread the string through each end and knot so it sits snugly at your chin. This chin cord will help keep your hat in place during your act.

5 Decorate your hat with pompoms, glitter, and ribbon to match your outfit.

Makeup
Magic

Your face makeup is an important part of your clown costume. Look in the mirror. What features do you want to exaggerate? Wiggle your face around to see what expressions you can make without makeup. Look for natural lines in your face that might serve as guidelines for your makeup.

Next, practice drawing clown faces (for face-drawing tips, see page 132). Draw some basic face shapes on a piece of paper, then experiment by adding different "makeup" features to each face. Change the shape of the mouth, eyebrows, nose, and cheek spots. What look do you like best?

GET DIGITAL!

With a digital camera and a basic illustrator or paint program, you can experiment with makeup on your computer! Have a friend take a close-up picture of your face. Then you can modify the picture on screen to add whiteface, cheek spots, a red mouth, black outlines, and other touches to preview your look.

Collecting Your Materials

Professional clowns use a kind of theatrical makeup called greasepaint. While this gives the most dramatic and long-lasting effects, greasepaint is difficult to work with, messy, and hard to find. A better choice is a good quality set of face paints. These are available at toy or hobby stores. During the Halloween season, you can usually find some inexpensive sets at a local drugstore.

CHECKLIST

- shower cap, headband, or hair clips
- an old shirt to cover your costume and keep it clean
- small brushes for fine details such as "teardrops" or lip outlines
- large brushes for bigger areas like forehead and cheeks
- face powder
- eyebrow pencil
- makeup sponges for blending and for applying large areas of color
- baby oil, baby shampoo, or makeup remover to wipe off mistakes and to clean up well afterwards
- facecloths, tissues, cotton swabs, and a hand towel

Putting on

Follow these ten tips from the pros for a perfect funny face.

Make sure your face is clean and dry before you start.

Use a shower cap, headband, or hair clips to keep your hair off your face while you work.

Are you planning to do a whiteface? Consider covering your neck and ears as well so that no flesh tone is visible.

Apply a light coat of makeup first. If you are doing a whiteface, make the first coat thin. Let it dry, then dab a second coat over the first. You may need to do three coats or more.

Use an eyebrow pencil to outline the areas you intend to highlight with makeup: your eyes, mouth, and cheeks, for instance.

Your Face

Test for **skin allergies** before you cover your face with makeup by testing just a small patch of skin first.

Start at the top of your forehead and work your way down to your chin. Cover your own eyebrows with face paint. Then draw new, more expressive eyebrows higher up.

Start with the lightest colors and let them dry completely before working your way up to the darkest. Work slowly and carefully so you don't smear the colors.

Keep the area between your nose and upper lip bare or white. This will help make your mouth stand out.

Use large, simple shapes and bold colors. Too many small details will not be visible to your audience.

Most Auguste clowns attach red ball noses on top of their makeup. If you don't have one, draw a red circle on the tip of your nose.

The Auguste Clown Face

1 Using the eyebrow pencil, outline large shapes around the features you want to accentuate: your eyes, mouth, and cheeks.

2 Exaggerate these features using white, red, or another color of face paint. Leave the rest of your face natural.

3 Outline the key features, such as your lips, with black.

4 Add details such as eyebrows or freckles.

5 Dust with face powder to help set the makeup so it won't smear.

The Pierrot Clown

1 Cover your entire face with white face paint. Let dry. Repeat as needed.

2 Using a fine brush or a makeup pencil, draw on details such as a small rosebud mouth, a red dot for a nose, and eyebrows. Maybe draw a teardrop or stick a glittery star on one cheek.

3 Keep your makeup delicate and subtle.

4 Dust with face powder to help set the makeup and keep it from smearing.

The Comedy Whiteface Clown

1 Cover your entire face with white face paint. Let dry. Repeat as needed.

2 Using the eyebrow pencil, outline large shapes around the features you want to accentuate, such as your eyes, mouth, and cheeks.

3 Exaggerate features using red or another color of face paint.

4 Outline the key features, such as your mouth, with black.

5 Add details like eyebrows or freckles.

6 Dust with face powder to help set the makeup and keep it from smearing.

YOU CRACKED THE CODE!

NO TWO ALIKE

Clowns have the right to protect their own unique look and act. This right is described in an unofficial "Code of Non-Infringement." This practice is of such a great importance that it is often referred to by clowns simply as "The Code."

In Britain, to make sure the code is honored, clowns have their own unique face makeup design painted onto an eggshell. No two eggs may be exactly alike!

Laff-Riot Recipes II

SCRUMPTIOUS SNOWBALLS

You'll Need

500 mL (2 cups)
finely shredded coconut

500 mL (2 cups)
graham cracker crumbs

250 mL (1 cup)
mini chocolate chips

1 can (300 mL/10 oz.)
condensed milk

You'll Also Need

measuring cups and spoons

pie plate • mixing bowl

wooden spoon

YIELD: 10-30 snowballs,
depending on size

PREP. TIME: 15 minutes

Who says making snowballs is just a recipe for trouble? Not you, when you have these sweet treats on hand.

1. Pour the shredded coconut in the pie plate. Set aside.

2. In the bowl, mix together the graham cracker crumbs, the chocolate chips, and the condensed milk. Stir well to combine.

3. Wash your hands. Using your fingers, grab a golf ball–sized lump of the mixture. Roll into a ball.

4. Roll each ball in the coconut.

5. For extra fun, make three balls in different sizes and squish them together to make a mini edible snowman.

6. Eat right away, or store in the fridge for later.

Clowning takes lots of energy. And boy does it make you ha-ha-hungry! Try this sampling of clown cuisine. Everything is fun to make and even more fun to eat.

YIELD:
12 necklaces

PREP. TIME:
15 minutes

JUICY JEWEL NECKLACES

You'll Need

1 bag of 12 licorice shoe strings

cereal or candy with a hole in the middle, mini pretzels, etc. to be the "jewels"

Does your clown costume need a little glamor? Jazz up your attire by making these nifty necklaces to wear and munch.

1 Thread your jewels onto your necklace.

2 Tie the two ends of the licorice together.

3 Wear. Eat when hungry.

77

A GRAND Entrance

How you enter the stage as a clown is important. Try these goofy greetings for a hilariously memorable "hello" to your audience.

The "Looking In" Gag

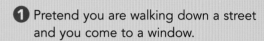

YOU'LL NEED

imagination

1. Pretend you are walking down a street and you come to a window.

2. Look through the window. Can you see the audience on the other side? Smile and wave.

3. Try to open the window. Struggle with the window. Finally raise the sash.

4. Put your hands on the imaginary windowsill and look out the window. Look down! Aaaagh—you're 75 stories up! Step back. Look scared.

5. Scratch your head. How will you get to the audience? Ask for help! Do this in a goofy way, either by miming gestures or by using words.

6. Take suggestions from the audience. Get them to encourage you to walk around the window. Finally do so.

7. Present yourself. Ta-dah! Here you are, ready to begin your act.

The "Climbing In" Gag

● ● ● ● ● ● ● ● ● ● ● ● ● ● ● ● ●

YOU'LL NEED
a real door frame

1 If there is a doorway between you and your "stage," use it for this dramatic entrance.

2 Pretend that the doorframe is lying on its side, and that one of the uprights is actually the bottom edge.

3 Stick your head in on an angle from the side through the doorway. See your audience. Wave hello.

4 "Climb" around the edge of the doorway, so that it looks as if you are climbing over the edge of a ledge.

5 Slide down the edge of the wall. Slip. Clutch the wall. Drag yourself around.

6 Fall onto the floor on the audience's side of the door.

7 Dust yourself off. Stand up and present yourself as if you have just accomplished a tremendous feat.

TRIPS and FALLS

If you want to be a clown, prepare to fall down. A lot. Knowing how to trip is an important clown skill, and guarantees a good laugh from your audience.

The Classic Trip

This gag will get your act off on the right foot.

YOU'LL NEED

a prop lying on the floor (optional)   noisemaker (optional)   dust cloth

1. Walk along in your chosen clown walk.

2. Is there an object on the stage you want to trip over? If so, head straight for it, but don't see it—perhaps you are waving to the audience. An imaginary object can work too.

3. When you arrive at your trip zone, step off onto one foot, just like a normal step. Bring the second foot up right behind your first foot so that the toe of your second foot touches the heel of your first foot.

4. Lean forward.

5. Hop.

6. Add a sound effect—maybe a horn (hidden in your pocket), or say "Oopsy-daisy!" or squeal.

7. Stop. Look at the spot you tripped over. Dust it off with your cloth. Walk away from it, checking it out over your shoulder.

8. If you tripped on an imaginary object, work it into your act by examining it, testing it, lifting it, moving it, opening it. Pretend, perhaps, it is a chair. Set it in a new place. Sit in your imaginary chair. Cross your legs. Then, oops! Fall to the floor. It's not real, right?

The Classic Pratfall

Practice this move on a soft rug or grassy area. Keep the area free of other objects, such as chairs, toys, or rocks.

● ●

1 Warm up your body before you practice. Jump around a bit to get your heart beating faster and your muscles loose. This will help prevent injury.

2 Squat down as if you are about to sit on the floor.

3 Roll backwards onto your back.

4 As soon as your backside hits the floor, slap the ground beside you with both hands. This will not only break your fall, but it will make a satisfying loud THUMP that will help make your fall more convincing.

5 Let your legs kick and splay out in a crazy way.

6 Roll forward into a sitting position, and show the audience your comical expression—embarrassment, confusion, or exaggerated pain.

SHAKING HANDS

Sometimes you will greet your audience members personally. Try these funny ways to say hello.

1 Pretend your hand gets stuck to theirs.

2 Pretend their hand is on fire! YE-OUCH!

3 Pretend the person whose hand you're shaking is so strong that they are squeezing your hand too hard! Add lots of moans and groans.

4 Each time the other person pumps your hand, jump up.

5 Pretend you are not shaking their hand. Keep talking, and keep shaking...and shaking...and shaking....

81

Silent Clown GAGS

No matter what kind of clown you are, having great body language will make your act. Communicating silently, through mime, is a great way to practice.

WITHOUT WORDS

The word mime comes from the same root as mimicry. It means to copy. You act out a scene by copying, or impersonating, an object, animal, or character—all without words. Before trying these activities in front of an audience, practice in front of a large mirror.

The Invisible Box

YOU'LL NEED

imagination

1. Pretend you are sitting on the floor inside a box that measures 1 m (3 ft.) tall by 1 m (3 ft.) wide.

2. Reach out. Touch the sides of the invisible box. Flatten your hands as if you're touching a flat surface.

3. Slide your hands along one side of the box. Rap on it with your knuckles. Lean forward and put your ear to it.

4. Move around the box. Show, through your actions, where the box borders are.

5. Reach up. Aha! The box top is open! Carefully climb out.

The Invisible Staircase

YOU'LL NEED

a sofa

a prop (optional)

1 Stand alongside a sofa, facing your audience.

2 Indicate to your audience that you need a prop—for example, a balloon—and that it is in the basement. This prop can be imaginary or real. If you decide to use a real prop, hide it behind the sofa before you begin your routine.

3 Pretend that there are stairs going down to the basement behind the sofa.

4 Go behind the sofa and fake walking down one step. Lower your body to mimic going down one stair. Your legs are hidden by the sofa so your audience will only see your upper body.

5 Take another step forward. At the same time, lower your body another 15 cm (6 in.). Keep your back straight. Your audience will see you seemingly walking down the stairs.

6 Keep going down until you are completely hidden by the sofa. Turn around and slowly walk back up the stairs, bringing the prop with you.

more Clown GAGS

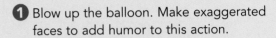

The Stubborn Balloon

YOU'LL NEED
a balloon

1. Blow up the balloon. Make exaggerated faces to add humor to this action.

2. When the balloon is blown up, tie it off and display it to the audience. Take a bow.

3. Now, move to place the balloon on the table. The balloon is stuck to your hand!

4. Try to remove it. It's so heavy! It won't move!

5. Try to push the balloon. Bend your arms to make it look like this is hard work. Cross your eyes and hold your breath so your face turns red.

6. With great effort, push the balloon to the tabletop. There! Remove one hand to wipe your brow in relief. Oh no! The balloon is suddenly light, and starts to fly away! Lift the balloon with your other hand in such a way that the balloon looks like it is pulling you.

7. Pretend that the balloon is rising in the air and about to lift you off the ground. Follow the balloon off stage, miming a frightened goodbye to the audience.

The Invisible Wall

YOU'LL NEED
a squeaky toy (optional)

1 Face the audience. Pretend you are walking toward them along a street when BONK! You smack into a wall.

2 Facing the audience, feel the invisible wall in front of you. Feel up and down, and from side to side.

3 Moving along the wall, come to something strange. Pull your hand away suddenly. Explore tentatively. It is a doorknob!

4 Mime examining the doorknob. If you put a squeaky toy in one pocket, you can make squeaking sounds as you finger the knob.

5 Turn the doorknob. Slowly lean back as you open the imaginary door toward you.

6 Look through the imaginary door. Oohh! You see the audience! Wave hello. Gingerly, step over the threshold of the door. Turn around and pull the door shut.

7 Face the audience again and take a bow. Wave goodbye, then turn around to walk away off stage.

8 Bonk! Smack into the wall once again and fall down. Crawl off stage, rubbing your aching head.

Ooof!

Clown Techniques for Every Act

Just like stand-up comics, clowns need to plan their acts. Over the next few pages, you'll find lots of great bits to fit into your act. As with a stand-up comedy routine, the bits of your clown act should link together to make a great show.

The Clown's Best Friend: The Secret Pocket

For some routines, secret pockets will come in handy to hold your props.

YOU'LL NEED

a vest, jacket, or pants into which you have permission to cut a hole and sew a hidden pocket

a square of fabric

regular scissors • pins

pinking shears (optional)

needle and colorful yarn

1. Decide where you want your pocket, and how big it will be. Cut the fabric to the right size.

2. Pin it in place on the outside of your jacket, vest, or pants. Try on the item of clothing and look in the mirror to ensure the pocket looks right with your outfit. Adjust size and position until you are satisfied.

3. Ask for an adult's help with this step. Unpin one or two sides of the pocket. Use the scissors to cut a small slit in your jacket, vest or pants underneath the pocket. If you have them, use the pinking shears to enlarge the slit (they'll help prevent the edges from unraveling). The slit should go all the way through the fabric, and be large enough that you can slip your fingers through it.

4. Pin the pocket back into place on all sides.

5. Use the yarn to sew the pocket into place. Sew only the two sides and the bottom—leave the opening at the top!

The Loose Thread Routine

1 Put the spool of thread into your undershorts. Yes, it feels funny, but you're a clown, right?

2 Take the loose end of thread and carefully feed it through the slit in your secret pocket so that the end is sticking out and over the pocket, and hanging loose from your outfit.

3 Sometime during your routine, pretend to just notice the loose thread hanging off your costume.

4 Point it out to the audience. Start to pull the thread to remove it from your costume. Of course, the thread is attached to an entire spool!

5 Keep pulling on it. The loose thread is getting longer and longer! Act surprised, fed-up, perplexed, annoyed, shocked.

6 Ask an audience member to help you out. Give him the thread. Let him pull and pull and pull. The thread keeps coming!

7 Get yourself all tangled up in the thread, rolling it around you when you are pulling.

*Shortcut: To do this without a Secret Pocket, thread a needle onto a spool and carefully place them into a regular pocket. Poke the needle out through the pocket material and pull thread through. Remove needle and let the loose thread dangle.

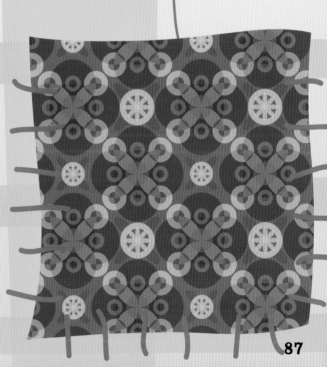

more Clown Techniques *for* Every Act

The "Airing Your Dirty Linens in Public" Routine

. . . .

YOU'LL NEED

a piece of string approximately 10 m (30 ft.) long

10–15 pieces of assorted clothing, preferably extra-large or extra-small sizes (consider underpants, socks, t-shirts, colorful handkerchiefs)

safety pins

your Secret Pocket (see page 86)

1 Make sure your largest item of clothing can fit through the slit in your Secret Pocket. If it won't slip through easily, either make the opening in your pocket larger or choose a smaller item of clothing.

2 Leave the first metre (3 ft.) of string empty. Using the safety pins, attach each item, spacing the clothes evenly along the rest of the string. Your finished prop will look like a clothesline.

3 Carefully roll up the string, starting with the clothed end. Keep the string and clothes from getting tangled. Stuff the ball of clothes into your underpants.

4 Pull the empty end of the string through the slit in your Secret Pocket. Tuck the end down into the pocket so you can reach it easily, but it remains hidden.

5 When you do the routine, come up with a reason for taking a piece of string from your pocket. Perhaps you need to tie it to the handle of your wagon.

6 Show the audience the string. Start to pull. Uh-oh! Here come the items of clothing!

7 Look shocked. Look embarrassed. Keep on pulling. Make your last item something especially funny like a large pair of boxer shorts or a bunch of silk flowers for extra laughs.

The Lost Leg Routine

YOU'LL NEED

a square of cloth or a scarf,
big enough to hold at your waist level
and still touch the floor

1. Tell the audience that you brought a picnic blanket and you're going to lay out a tasty picnic as it's such a nice day.

2. Unfold the cloth in front of you. Make sure it drapes over the toes of your shoes. Keep up your patter by describing the food, where your picnic will be, whatever fits in with your routine.

3. While you are talking, secretly take one foot out of your shoe. Bend your leg up at the knee.

4. Keep talking, gradually allowing the cloth to lift a bit so your audience can see one leg and one empty shoe.

5. Look down, over the cloth, in surprise! Where did your leg go?

6. Look around for your leg.

7. Take away the cloth to show your audience your trick. Laugh with them at your own silly trick.

More Clown Techniques for Every Act

The Disastrous Decorator Routine

For this classic bit, you will pretend you are about to paint or wallpaper a room.

YOU'LL NEED

double-sided tape • a paintbrush

a roll of paper • a bucket • a table

1 Put some double-sided tape on the handle of the brush, and another piece on the paper. Place brush in the bucket.

2 Carry your roll of paper, bucket, and brush onstage. Set the paper down on the table, and the bucket on the floor.

3 Unroll the paper. Let it roll closed again. Do this several times, getting more and more exasperated.

4 Get a good idea: put the bucket on the paper to hold it in place. Put your hand down on the paper. It gets stuck!

5 Grab the bucket to pry yourself loose. Get your hand "stuck" to the bucket!

6 Unstick yourself with difficulty. Take out the brush. Of course your hand gets stuck to the brush instead! Try to fling it off.

7 Give up. Throw everything on the floor. Somehow, get your foot stuck in the bucket. Clomp off stage with the paper and brush stuck to your hand and the bucket on your foot.

Shortcut: You can get yourself totally stuck using nothing but masking tape! For your act, "break" something. This can even be an imaginary prop. "Repair" the break by taping it. Of course, you wind up getting yourself all stuck in the tape!

The Classic Fly Routine

YOU'LL NEED

an assortment of your own unbreakable props that you may knock over

a giant fly swatter (optional) made from a ruler and bristol board

1 Start your routine by pretending to get comfy in a bed or a chair.

2 Suddenly, you hear it: the annoying buzz of a fly. Follow the motion of the fly with your head and eyes. You will need to exaggerate.

3 Cross your eyes. The fly has come to rest on your nose.

4 Swat the fly! Kapowie! You hit yourself so hard you fall on your keester! Use your pratfall technique (page 81) for a big laugh.

5 Get angry. Stand up. Go back to your chair. There is that fly again!

6 Follow the fly with your eyes and body. Start chasing it. Keep swatting at it. Cause lots of damage as you go, knocking over props, etc.

7 Go offstage. Get your giant "fly swatter," if you have one.

8 Chase the fly. Miss. Knock over more of your props.

9 Chase the fly offstage. Make a loud thwacking sound several times.

10 Come back on stage, looking triumphant. Sit back down. Get comfy. Then look up in terror. It's a giant fly! Run off the stage.

more Clown Techniques *for* Every Act

The Hat Routine

Your hat is alive!
Use it in your routine.

YOU'LL NEED

a hat
with a brim

1 Raise your hat to the audience. It suddenly flies off your head! How?! Hold it on both sides of the brim, then lightly flick it up with your fingers.

2 Grab the hat and jam it back on your head. Flick it a few more times.

3 Let the hat fall on the floor. Make it look like it is jumping away from you by secretly kicking it with your toe as you bend to pick it up.

4 Use your hat in different ways. Hug it like it's your best friend. Maybe pretend there's a raw egg in it when you put it back on.

Hat-Juggling Trick

YOU'LL NEED

a hat with a firm brim

1 Stand with your feet planted about hip-width apart. Using your dominant hand (your right hand if you are right-handed, your left if you are left-handed), hold the hat by the brim out in front of you. Your hand should be extended about 30 cm (12 in.), at waist height. The inside of the hat should be facing you. Your thumb should be on the top of the brim.

2 Flip the hat up in front of you, releasing it at about shoulder height, when your hand is parallel to the floor. It should make a complete revolution in the air.

3 If you toss the hat correctly, it should spin up in the air and come down—plop!—right on your head. Keep your eye on the hat and bend your knees to help position yourself so the hat lands correctly. You may have to jut your neck slightly forward. A little practice and you'll be able to do this move every time.

The Classic Wire-Walker Routine

It's best to practice this one outside on the grass, using patio furniture chairs.

YOU'LL NEED

two light,
straight-backed chairs

around 2 m (6 ½ ft.)
of string

1 Set up the two chairs back to back, about 3 m (10 ft.) apart.

2 Tie the string to the back of the first chair. Cross the stage to the second. Pull the string so the first chair falls down.

3 Set it back up again. Repeat a few times.

4 Cross the stage more cautiously, making sure that the string is long enough to reach the second chair. Turn abruptly to make sure the first chair is still standing. The motion pulls the chair down.

5 Pretend you don't notice the chair falling down. Tie the string to the second chair. Turn around, and express shock that the first chair is on the ground!

6 Go back to the first chair, and stand it up so it pulls the second chair down.

7 Pick up chair two. Chair one falls down again.

8 Finally, collapse with exhaustion. Sit on the floor between the two chairs. Scratch your head.

9 Get a bright idea. Bring the chairs closer together so the string is pulled taut but they can both stand up. Bow!

10 Next show your audience that you are a highwire walker and you are going to cross the wire between the two chairs.

11 Act like you're about to step up onto the string. Pull your foot back in terror, biting your nails.

12 Get another bright idea. Move the chairs closer together so the string is lying on the floor. With great drama, walk along the string *on the ground*, miming a daring highwire act. Bow.

Daffy Dictionary

Every profession uses its own slang. Check out this collection of clowning terms so you can sound like a pro.

Boss clown: The head clown, responsible for coordinating the routines in a show.

Bump a nose: Clown version of the phrase "break a leg." Used to wish another performer good luck before they go on stage.

Caring clown: A clown who works in hospitals, hospices, or nursing homes to help cheer the sick.

Clown alley: Originally, the term referred to the narrow alley in a circus tent where the clowns kept their costume trunks and props. Now the term is used for a group or club of clowns.

Dying or sudden death: Terms used when a clown's routine falls flat while he or she is on stage.

First of May: A clown working his or her first season in the circus.

Hobo: Clown style based on the hobos that rode the rails (stowed away on trains) during the Depression era. They usually wear tattered clothes, and have a black or gray smudged beard and soot marks on their faces.

Jam session: When many clowns gather together to share information and ideas.

Joey: A clown.

Producing clown: A clown who is responsible for writing new routines. May also be the boss clown.

Production gag: A gag usually performed by a large group of clowns, directed by a producing clown. An example would be the famous "stuffing clowns into a car" routine.

OPEN WIDE, AND SAY "AHHH-HA-HA-HA!"

Many hospitals actually employ clowns. In 1986, Big Apple Circus, based in New York, established the first Intensive "Clown Care" Unit. Clowns go into hospitals to entertain patients and take their minds off of their illnesses. Other organizations around the world quickly followed suit. Today, there are "Clown Doctors" practicing all over the world.

Only Class Clowns Here

Can you imagine a school in which every student is a class clown? There are lots of them all over the world: the Jacques Lecoq International Theatre School in Paris, for example, and the Dell'Arte International School of Physical Theatre in California.

Partnering Up to Clown

When you work with a partner, one of you will act as the straight player, while the other gets the gag (see page 41). Make sure your brilliant act has these surefire elements:

(see page 41)

THE ENTRANCE
One or both clowns enter in such a way that the audience can instantly "get" each character. The shy clown tiptoes in timidly; the brash clown struts in arrogantly, for example.

THE MEETING
To begin the routine, the two clowns meet, or the clowns "meet" an object that is the main prop in the routine. The meeting can also be a discovery—say, one clown learns that the other is playing a trick on him.

The Classic Mirror Routine

To make this routine really shine, practice the improv activity Mirror, Mirror (page 52).

YOU'LL NEED

a horn or other honking noisemaker (optional)

❶ Clown 1 goes up to an imaginary mirror, looks in it, straightens his tie or hat and walks offstage.

❷ Clown 2 sneaks on stage. She lets the audience know she is going to play a trick on Clown 1. She mimes removing the mirror, and placing an empty frame in its place. She puts her hand through the frame to show the audience there isn't a mirror there.

❸ Clown 1 returns and passes by the mirror. This time, Clown 2 stands facing Clown 1 on the other side of the "mirror."

❹ Clown 1 sees his reflection. He looks different! He stops, takes a closer look. Clown 2 copies his motions exactly.

❺ Clown 1 cannot believe what he is seeing. He rubs his eyes. In unison, so does Clown 2. Every time Clown 1 moves, Clown 2 moves in exectly the same way, as a mirror reflection.

❻ Finally, Clown 1 honks his own nose. Clown 2 responds by reaching through the frame and honking Clown 1's nose, too— through the "mirror!"

THE CONFLICT

Like all good drama, there must be a basic conflict. In a duo routine, there should be a conflict between the two clowns. For example, one wants to accomplish a task, while the other just wants to have fun.

RESOLUTION

The conflict mounts until the tension is unbearable. It must be resolved on stage for a satisfying ending, by having the clowns solve the problem.

EXIT The exit is usually a chase, in keeping with the style of the rest of the routine.

IDEAS

Try out these ideas for your own original clown duet.

• Pretend you are firefighters, putting out a small fire.

• Pretend you are dogcatchers, and the dogs have gotten away.

• Pretend you have to give a speech, but you both forgot your glasses and you can't read it!

• Pretend you are a waiter and a customer in a crowded restaurant.

• Pretend you are in love with the other clown, who isn't interested.

The Classic Painters' or Cleaners' Routine

YOU'LL NEED

mops • buckets • paintbrushes • confetti

Both clowns enter with buckets and paintbrushes, or buckets and mops. They are going to get to work. But Clown 1 is such a klutz! She keeps getting everything all wrong. (You can use elements from the Disastrous Decorator routine, page 90: she gets stuck in the paint; she spills the water, and the other clown slips; she knocks him over with the mop.) When Clown 2 stands up, he gets knocked down with the other end of the mop. He can't stand it. He threatens Clown 1. Clown 1 gets mad. Clown 2 throws water over Clown 1 (the bucket has confetti in it, not water!). Exasperated, Clown 2 chases Clown 1 offstage.

Tips from the Pros

Get hold of a CD that includes some circus-style music, and try playing it during your routine to add to the effect. You can also add humor to the routine by using the famous clown Grock's technique of trying to play an instrument upside down (see page 65), with the strings, or holes of the woodwind, hidden from the musician's sight.

How to JUGGLE

Juggling is a great skill that can help get your act rolling, fill in during lulls, and keep up interest while you tell jokes or while a partner is changing costume.

STARTING OUT

The best way to learn how to juggle is to practice with colored handkerchiefs or squares of fabric. They move more slowly through the air than balls, and are easier to grab.

Juggling Bags

Try these handy homemade ones.

YOU'LL NEED

3 child-sized socks, in different colors (referred to here as red, yellow, and blue)

750 mL (3 cups) uncooked rice

3 rubber bands, or needle and thread

● ● ● ● ● ● ● ● ● ● ● ● ●

1 Fill each sock with 250 mL (1 cup) of rice—it should reach to the ankle.

2 Wind a rubber band around the neck of the sock to seal it closed. The band should be very tight, so no rice can fall out, or use strong thread to sew the socks shut.

PHASE 1 The Single Bagger

1. Hold the red bag in your right hand. Look straight ahead.

2. Toss it up in the air so it hits an imaginary point just above your left eye. Don't look at the bag, or your hands!

3. Catch the bag in your left hand.

4. Repeat until you can hit the imaginary spot over and over again, and catch the bag without looking.

5. When you can do this well, go on to Phase 2.

PHASE 3 The Triple Bagger

1. Hold the red and yellow bags in your right hand, and blue in your left.

2. Toss the red bag as before, to the imaginary point above your left eye. When the red bag hits the point, toss the blue bag lightly over to your right hand.

3. While the blue bag is crossing and the red bag is dropping, toss the yellow bag to the imaginary point above your left eye. Catch the red bag in your left hand. Catch the blue bag in your right.

4. Now simply continue, tossing the bags from your right hand to the point above your left eye, and gently passing the bags in your left hand over to your right.

PHASE 2 The Double Bagger

1. Hold the red bag in your right hand, and blue in your left. Toss the red bag as before—without looking at the bag or your hands!

2. When you release the red bag, toss the blue to an imaginary point above your right eye.

3. Catch the red bag in your left hand. Catch the blue bag in your right hand.

4. When you have mastered this motion, try tossing both bags back and forth in a rhythm. When you can do 100 tosses without dropping anything, you are ready for Phase 3.

Tips from the Pros

Don't worry if your juggling skills take a while to develop. If you drop a juggling bag in a routine, break into loud, overblown tears. Or let the bag drop, and continue juggling with the rest. When you finish, take a deep bow as if you succeeded terrifically. You're sure to get big laughs even if your juggling stinks.

Easier said than done? Of course! But with a little practice, the timing and positioning of your hands will become easier. Eventually, it will become automatic. You'll be juggling in your sleep.

Spooky Pranks

Practical

Doggone It!

Outdoor Fun...

Oh, My Aching Head!

Jokes

Laff-Riot Recipes

...and Frolic

Get Practical!

Sure, you can get laughs by telling a joke or dressing up in big shoes and a funny wig. But nothing, absolutely nothing, and I mean N-U-T-H-I-N-K, is funnier than a perfectly prepared, excellently executed practical joke. Whether it's April Fools' Day or just an ordinary Tuesday, check out these hilarious practical jokes.

What makes a good practical joke?

Like all humor, the best of the best rely on surprise. It fools you into thinking one thing, then delivers something completely different.

What makes a bad one?

Bad practical jokes cause harm. They make other people feel bad, or can even cause injury. No serious funster ever wants to pull a lame prank like that.

FOAMING AT THE MOUTH

Think there's no place for practical jokes in high society? Think again! In stuffy Victorian England, the Duchess of Marlborough had the habit of mixing slices of soap in with the cheese at her elegant parties. It is said that she enjoyed watching her refined guests swallow down the soap rather than display bad manners by spitting it out!

No Use Crying Over Spilled....
AAARGH!

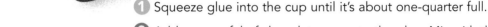

This mess-free practical joke always gets a great reaction!

YOU'LL NEED

a short, squat paper cup (the kind ice cream is served in)

wood glue

chocolate syrup

waxed paper

plastic spoon

*WARNING
Keep away from small children. Toxic if ingested.

1. Squeeze glue into the cup until it's about one-quarter full.

2. Add a spoonful of chocolate syrup to the glue. Mix with the plastic spoon. Add more syrup until the mixture is the color of chocolate ice cream.

3. Lay a sheet of waxed paper on a flat surface. Choose a workspace where your project can remain undisturbed for a drying period of up to one week.

4. Carefully lay the cup down on the waxed paper. Allow the mixture to spill out of the cup onto the waxed paper, forming a nice, chocolatey puddle.

5. Lightly place the bowl of the spoon in the puddle. It should look like an ice cream cup has tipped over, spilling out the melting ice cream and the spoon onto the waxed paper.

6. Allow your creation to dry. Be patient. It can take up to a week. Don't poke at it before it is completely dry or you'll mess it up.

7. When it is dry, the "spill" will be hard. You will then be able to peel it off the waxed paper and place your creation somewhere an ice cream spill shouldn't be.

8. Wait. Sooner or later you will hear the telltale shriek that means your victim has found it.

103

Doggone It!

You're sure to get laughs when you walk your invisible dog. If you don't have an old dog leash and collar to use, skip ahead to the instructions under "Making It from Scratch."

YOU'LL NEED

wire hanger

wire cutter pliers

old fabric dog leash and fabric dog collar you have permission to use

duct tape

white glue

bowl

waxed paper

1. Have an adult help you with this—to straighten out the wire hanger into a line. Use the pliers to unwind the closure at the hook of the hanger. Hold one part of the wire steady by clamping it with the tips of the pliers, and twist the rest of the wire with the other hand. To smooth out any last bumps, you can run the pliers along the hanger, clamping and opening as you go.

2. Lay the dog leash on a flat surface. Lay the straightened wire on top of the leash.

3. Unroll a strip of duct tape and tape the wire to the leash. Trim the wire as needed.

4. Next, pour some glue, about 60 mL (1/4 cup), into the bowl. Put the dog collar into the bowl and smush it around until it is completely saturated with the glue. Add more glue if you need it.

5. When the collar is nicely gloopy, remove it from the bowl. Shape the collar into a round circle, then lay it on a sheet of waxed paper. Allow the collar to dry completely. When the glue dries, the collar will have stiffened into a hard ring.

6. Attach the collar to the leash. Go on to "Polishing Your Prank" (at right).

Making It from Scratch

. . . .

YOU'LL NEED

wire hanger

wire cutter pliers

2 pieces of felt, each 28 cm
(11 in.) x 36 cm (14 in.)

ruler

white glue

small metal buckle or button
snaps (optional)

WOOF?

1. Follow step 1 on page 104 to straighten out your wire hanger.

2. Cut four strips of felt, each measuring approximately 2.5 cm (1 in.) wide by 33 cm (13 in.) long.

3. Lay two strips of felt, end to end on a flat surface to form a single strip measuring 2.5 cm (1 in.) wide by 66 cm (26 in.) long. Spread white glue on both strips.

4. Lay the straightened wire lengthwise on top of the gluey felt. Then lay the remaining pieces of felt on top of the wire. This will make a long, narrow felt-and-wire sandwich. Press together to seal. Let glue dry.

POLISHING YOUR PRANK

Now that you have completed your invisible dog's leash, you will need to perfect your invisible dog–walking skills.

Look at yourself in a full-length mirror, holding the leash and collar. Adjust until it looks very convincing that there's a dog at the end.

Practice walking with the leash. It should look as if your invisible dog is prancing along beside you, or pulling your arm as he runs ahead!

When you take your dog act out for a walk, talk in a baby voice to your pooch. And don't forget to stop now and then to let "Buffy" sniff.

5. Form the collar by bending one end of the felt-covered wire into a circle about 12 cm (5 in.) wide. Glue the felt ring closed to finish the collar. To make the collar look more realistic, you can decorate by gluing on a metal buckle or snaps.

6. Straighten and shape the rest of the felt-covered wire to form the long part of the leash. You may want to attach a felt loop at the top end to make a soft handle.

7. Go on to "Polishing Your Prank" (at left).

Oh, My Aching Head!

The his super sight gag is extremely quick and easy to make.

YOU'LL NEED

wire hanger • wire cutter pliers

ruler • plastic straw

tape • tracing paper

black construction paper

pencil • scissors

1 Follow step 1 of the Doggone It! activity on page 104 to straighten out the wire hanger. Ask a grownup to help you with this step.

2 Hold the wire horizontally across the top of your head. The middle of the wire should be centered on the top of your head. Holding the wire in place, curve it down around your head. Squeeze it into shape until it fits like a hairband, with two straight ends sticking out horizontally from ear level. The wire will look like this:

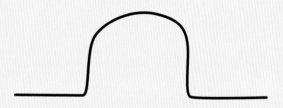

3 With an adult's help, use the wire cutters to cut the ends of the wire so that each straight segment measures approximately 9 cm (3 3/4 in.) long.

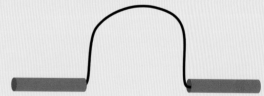

4 Cut the straw in half. Slip one half over each straight end of the wire. The straw should completely cover the wire, with a little bit of straw left over at the tips. Trim the wire again if necessary. Fasten the straws in place with tape if they slide off.

5 Trace the arrowhead design below. Cut out. Then trace around shape onto black construction paper. Cut out. Make notches to cut in where shown.

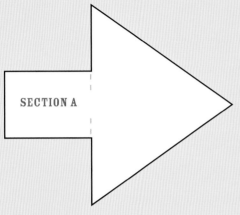

SECTION A

7 For feathers for the other end of the arrow, trace the design below, then copy onto construction paper. Cut out. Cut slits to make "feathers," and notches to roll Section B. Insert into the straw end. Tape.

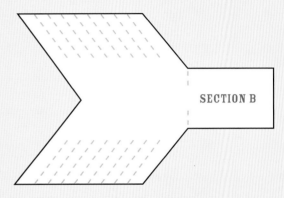

SECTION B

6 Roll up Section A. When rolled up, it should fit inside the end of the straw. Fit the arrowhead in place at the end of one of the straws. Tape to secure if necessary.

8 Enter a room where your friends are gathered. Complain that you have a headache, but you just don't know why!

WHAT A HEADACHE!

Laff-Riot Recipes IV

"POACHED EGGS"
with "Bacon"

You'll Need

1 pound cake

796 mL (28 oz.) can peach halves in light syrup or juice

1 can whipped cream

1 roll of red fruit-roll snacks

You'll Also Need

knife

4 plates

This egg-cellent recipe will have people asking for eggs-tra helpings.

1 Carefully slice the cake into 2.5 cm (1 in.) thick slices to resemble toast. Ask a grownup for help with this step. Place one slice on each of the plates.

2 Spritz a blob of whipped cream in the center of your "toast" to represent the egg white.

3 Lay one peach half, flat side down, into the blob of "egg white." This will be your yolk.

4 Cut two strips of the fruit-roll candy to lay alongside your "toast." This will be your bacon.

YIELD: Serves 4

PREP. TIME: 15 minutes

Why not bring some sneaky techniques into the kitchen to fool the eye and tickle the funnybone?

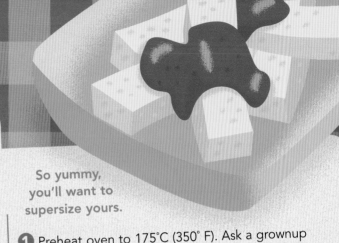

POUND CAKE "FRIES"
with Raspberry "Ketchup"

You'll Need

1/4 loaf pound cake

340 g (12 oz.) bag frozen raspberries, thawed, or 500 mL (2 cups) fresh berries

30 mL (2 tbsp.) water or lemon juice (optional)

30 mL (2 tbsp.) confectionery (icing) sugar

You'll Also Need

knife • cookie sheet • tongs

blender or food processor

measuring cups and spoons

fine mesh strainer • mixing bowl

rubber spatula • spoon

2 french fry containers (from a fast-food joint) or a plate

YIELD: Serves 2
PREP. TIME: 30 minutes

So yummy, you'll want to supersize yours.

1. Preheat oven to 175°C (350° F). Ask a grownup for help using the oven, knife, and blender.

2. Cut the pound cake into 1 cm (1/2 in.) thick slices. Then cut each slice into 1 cm (1/2 in.) wide strips.

3. Arrange cake strips in a single layer on a cookie sheet. Toast in oven until brown, about 5 minutes. Use the tongs to turn the strips onto their sides. Toast until remaining two sides are browned. Watch carefully. This will only take a few minutes.

4. Remove from the oven, and let strips cool. Then arrange the "fries" in the boxes or on the plates.

5. To make the "ketchup," puree raspberries in a blender or food processor. If the mixture is lumpy, add 15–30 mL (1–2 tbsp.) of water or lemon juice. Add the sugar, 5 mL (1 tsp.) at a time, to taste.

6. Place the strainer over the bowl. Pour the puree through to remove seeds from your "ketchup." Use the spatula to push the puree through. Throw away the seeds from the strainer. Spoon "ketchup" from bowl over top of the fries. Serve!

OUTDOOR FUN and FROLIC

Things Are Looking Up!

Get a couple of friends together to try out this great joke some place where there are lots of passersby (like in the schoolyard). You'll get a giggle watching different people's reactions.

. . . .

YOU'LL NEED

at least one friend
(but the more, the merrier)

nothing but acting skills

1 Choose a spot where there are tall buildings (like your school) and/or trees.

2 Gather your crew around. Have everyone look up. Occasionally, point up, like there is something really outrageous in a tree or on top of the buildings.

3 Watch for the reactions of people passing by. Giggle.

Money Mania

Enrich your repertoire with this priceless prank.

YOU'LL NEED

paper money,
in any denomination

fishing line

tape

1. Tape one end of the fishing line to the paper money.

2. Lay the bill in a hallway—somewhere you know your brother or sister will pass by, for example.

3. Roll out enough line so that you can stand out of sight but can still see the bill—like behind a bedroom door. Keep hold of the line!

4. Wait until someone walking by spots the money on the ground.

5. As they reach for the bill, quickly yank the fishing line to pull the bill out of their reach. Do this in a few quick, short, strokes, and the bill will look like its fluttering in a breeze.

6. Keep pulling it out of the victim's reach until they catch on to the gag.

7. Repeat on new victims.

Spooky

THE CORPSE'S
Finger

This is so disgusting and realistic even your mom will love it!

• •

YOU'LL NEED

a cardboard gift box (a bit longer than the length from the fingertip to the bottom of the middle knuckle of your middle finger), with lid

the cotton that comes with the box, and maybe some extra cotton from a cotton ball

red food coloring • scissors

chalk in different colors

1. Cut a hole in the bottom of the box. It should be close to one end, and large enough to put your middle finger through.

2. Test your creation by slipping your finger into the hole. You should be able to hold the box in the palm of that hand, with your finger resting comfortably inside the box.

3. Fit the cotton around your finger to hide the hole in the box.

4. Dribble red food coloring onto the cotton to simulate blood.

5. Using the chalk, color your finger a creepy bluish, grayish, greenish, blackish white. It is supposed to belong to a corpse.

PRANKS

6 Put the lid on the box. Put the box in your pocket.

7 Tell your friends that you found a finger belonging to a corpse in the woods. Tell them how gross it is. Tell them how hard it was for you to get the courage to pick up the finger and put it in a box. Tell them that you have the box in your pocket.

8 When your victims ask to see the finger, slip your chalky finger into the box. Then bring it out of your pocket. Use your other hand to remove the lid.

9 When your friends start to study the finger, wiggle it ever so slightly. The screams will be loud enough to, er, wake the dead.

⇒ Eeep! ⇐

THE
Monster
IN YOUR HOUSE

YOU'LL NEED

a rubber glove

fake fur

glue

scissors

fake fingernails
(you can use cardboard)

114

1. Cut the fake fur into a hand shape so that it covers the top of the glove. Don't worry—it doesn't have to be perfectly neat. It's a monster hand, right? Glue the fur piece onto the glove.

2. Glue the fake nails to the fingertips, on top of the fur. You have now created a monster hand.

3. Tell your victim that a monster has moved into your house. His name is "Wally." Of course, your friend will not believe you. Tell him you will introduce him to Wally right now.

4. Walk through a doorway into another room. This is the room where "Wally" lives. Stand right in the doorway where your friend can see you.

5. Turn sideways in the doorway to talk to Wally. Hold out your hand, like you are extending it towards the monster. Say something like, "Hey, Wally! Come on and meet my friend. No? What's the matter with you? Why do you look so angry? Hey, Wally! Cut it out!"

6. Then jerk your body so it looks like Wally has just yanked on your extended arm. Step past the doorway so your friend can't see you. Quickly put on the monster rubber glove. Make banging noises and yell things like "Ouch! Stop!" while you get the glove on.

7. Step back into the doorway. This time, face your victim straight on. Make sure the arm wearing the glove is still hidden behind the edge of the doorframe.

8. Bend your gloved arm and bring it across your body so that only the glove shows. Your elbow and the rest of your arm are still hidden by the doorway; it will look like the monster hand is reaching across you from where he is sitting behind the door.

9. Then let the monster hand pull you away from the door again.

10. Quickly take off the glove. In a stern voice say, "That's enough of that nonsense, Wally. Back in your cage!" Make banging and growling sounds (use two spoons to make metallic clanging, like the sound of a cage door shutting). Make one final loud bang, and then go back to join your friend.

11. Wipe off your hands and say, "Whew! He gets so cranky when he hasn't been fed. Maybe we better wait for another time to introduce you two." Undoubtedly, your friend will agree.

115

Mix 'n' Match

Comic Strips

Drawing Characters

Flipbook Animation

Drawing Animals

and
CartOOns

Cartoon
Shortcuts

Get Ready to Draw

So maybe you're not really the practical joker type. You'd rather get your giggles without drawing attention to yourself. You'd rather just, well, draw. In that case, why not try your hand at cartooning? You don't have to be a great artist to be a whizz-bang cartoonist. But you do need to know how to turn your drawings to master-pieces of high comic art. Ready? On your markers, get set, draw!

How did comics get their start? Probably with cave dwellers drawing funny stick figures by firelight. But it was the ancient Egyptians who drew the earliest known cartoons. Ancient Egyptian carvings show many goofy scenes of animals behaving like people and people behaving like animals. They were also fond of "earthy" humor (this is a polite way of saying potty jokes). Ancient Sumerians, Greeks, and Romans all used cartoons or humorous pictures in paintings and decoration. The Greeks were fond of drawing dog-faced monkeys on their pottery. The Romans liked silly pictures of tiny people with big round heads.

Careless Pictures

The word manga, a Japanese term for comic book, was used in the eighteenth century by the celebrated artist Hokusai. He made up the word from two Chinese characters that roughly meant "careless pictures" to describe his own doodles!

HOORAY FOR PRINTING!

Japanese scrolls dating from the twelfth century told stories using pictures. They were extremely funny, but very few people saw them. Producing each scroll took many years of work, and only the rich could afford them. When printing was invented in the seventeenth century, the humorous scroll stories were among the first to be reproduced. It wasn't long before they became wildly popular throughout Japan—the first mass-produced "comic books."

119

DRAWING
THROUGH TIME

It was a long way to go from the Japanese story-pictures of the 1600s to the newspaper comic strips of today. Even after movable type printing was invented, drawings were too hard to reproduce and too expensive to include in newspapers. Instead, early cartoonists sold their humorous drawings in the form of prints.

It was not until 1873 that technology caught up with art. A new process, line photo engraving, made it faster and easier to reproduce illustrations on a printing press. Cartoons could at last be included in daily newspapers, and they became a very popular feature. There was no turning back—the newspaper cartoon was here to stay.

FROM COMIC STRIP TO COMIC BOOK

The first comic book was a collection of color comics from the Hearst newspapers. It had a cardboard cover and sold for 50 cents—a lot of money at the time. The all-paper comic book did not appear until the 1930s. At first, superheroes were the most popular subjects, featuring characters like Superman, Prince Valiant, the Phantom, Captain Marvel, and Dick Tracy.

FEELING SICK?

Maybe you read too many funnies. The nickname that pros use for the daily comic strip is "Gag-a-Day."

EVERYTHING ARCHIE

The first *Archie* comic was published in 1941. Today, *Archie* is enjoyed by an astonishing 1.25 million readers every month! Archie creator John Goldwater wanted to create a character who was not a clown or a superhero, but just an ordinary person, living a "real" life. Goldwater based Archie on a friend named Archie, from high school. The character of Jughead, he says, was based on himself!

THE U.S. POSTAL SERVICE ISSUED A POSTAGE STAMP COMMEMORATING THE *100TH* ANNIVERSARY OF THE COMIC STRIP IN *1996.*

THE WORLD'S LONGEST COMIC STRIP IS *88.9* METRES (*292* FEET) LONG!

WHAT'S THE DIFFERENCE BETWEEN A "CARTOON" AND A "COMIC?" NOTHING! BOTH WORDS ARE USED TO REFER TO A HUMOROUS ILLUSTRATION.

WORKING FOR PEANUTS?

Charles Schulz was the creator of the *Peanuts* comic strip, one of the most popular strips of all time. *Peanuts* first appeared on October 2, 1950, and featured the hapless Charlie Brown and his dog Snoopy. *Peanuts* ran for nearly 50 years without interruption, appearing in over 75 countries, and spawning dozens of books, TV shows, movies, and even a stage show.

The **RULES** of the **ROAD**

When you draw cartoons, the first thing to remember is that all comics are jokes. Like other jokes, they depend on certain basic elements to make them funny. There needs to be a **setup** and a **punch line**. And there needs to be an element of surprise, or a **twist**.

The pictures and the words of a cartoon are both important. A really funny picture might be good enough for a laugh, but in the best cartoons, the text and pictures work together. Good writers make good cartoonists.

READ ME FIRST.

READ ME NEXT.

MOVING IN THE RIGHT *DIRECTION*

Cartoons, like jokes that you tell, also have direction. A joke begins with a setup, then moves toward the punch line. In a cartoon, the setup is usually the picture, and the text provides the punch line. How do you make sure readers see these parts of your cartoon in the right order? A cartoonist needs to arrange the cartoon elements properly.

Since English speakers read from left to right, and from the top to the bottom of the page, your cartoon will also read from left to right, and top to bottom. Place the elements that you want readers to see first in the upper left of your cartoon. Elements you want them to notice or read last should go at the bottom right.

I'M LAST, BUT USUALLY THE FUNNIEST.

Cartoon Formats

Panel Cartoon

...SO THE CHIHUAHUA SAYS TO THE GREAT DANE...

Whoofer's first experience with a funny bone.

1 The first is the **panel cartoon**. The panel cartoon is a single frame. It usually has a caption beneath the picture.

SHORT AND SWEET

The pros follow this rule: the shorter the caption, the better the joke. Single panel cartoons should have captions of no more than 12 words. Captions and dialogue should never repeat something already shown by the picture, or that would be better illustrated than described.

2 The second cartoon type is the multi-panel, or **comic strip**. The strip is usually made up of three to four panels. The first panel sets the scene and initiates the action. The next panel presents the setup line. And the final panel contains the punch line. **Tip:** When creating a comic strip, you should break down your story into chunks that can be clearly illustrated within each panel.

Comic Strip

PANEL VS. STRIP

The panel cartoon, like a snapshot, captures a single moment in time. It is the cartoon equivalent of a one-liner. The comic strip can tell a more complicated story. Each panel is a separate scene. The space between panels, called the alley or gutter, tells the reader that there is a change in time or place.

WHAT a CHARACTER!

Want to know the secrets to creating great characters? They need to be **recognizable**. At a glance, readers need to know if they are looking at a toddler or an alien, a pig or a duck. They also need to be **understandable**. They need to show their emotions and movements clearly. And they need to **display personality** —unique attributes that make characters one of a kind.

In cartoons, readers only have a few seconds to "get" the joke. They need to instantly identify the characters and be able to draw conclusions about their personalities, motivations, and actions.

CREATE YOUR OWN CHARACTERS

To make their characters instantly recognizable, cartoonists rely on stereotypes. For example, glasses are often used to convey the idea of "brainy." Big muscles and lots of hair suggest "caveman." A suit indicates a business executive. An outfit with stripes says "prisoner."

How would you create characters based on these stereotypes?

- harried parent
- school jock
- lazy student
- computer nerd
- bully
- snob
- teacher's pet
- artsy type
- math whiz
- nervous Nellie

Mix 'n' Match

Which words from the list on the left match to the cartoon stereotype on the right?

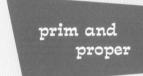

prim and proper

capable, can-do

dopey

sinister

Drawing Characters

Think about some of your favorite cartoon characters. What makes them appealing? Do you like the expressions on their faces, or their soft, rounded shapes? Do they remind you of real people, or do they seem completely wacky?

How to Get a Head

A great way to practice your drawing technique is to create cartoon heads without bodies. The arms and legs will stick out directly from the head. Since they have no bodies, you will need to pay extra attention to your characters' facial features and the props they hold to get the effect you want. You can make your characters wild and crazy or keep them simple. Both are effective and fun.

TRICKS OF THE TRADE

Cartoonists know that drawing a large head on a small body makes a character seem friendlier and more child-like. On the other hand, a superhero or an authority figure will seem more imposing if he or she has a larger, longer body, and a smaller head.

Cartoonists also exaggerate. They make eyes extra large or extra small. They stretch noses into ski-jump peaks, or transform them into outlandish snouts. Arms can be extra-long rubber bands, and feet can be giant pancakes. Muscles pop, tongues slurp, hair shoots in all directions. Exaggerate your characters' features to give them instant presence and power. Try the improv game "Happy Birthday Box" on page 53 to help you develop your own exaggeration skills.

129

Stand-Out Characters

Try applying some of these tricks of proportion to help make your own characters really stand out in a crowd.

A normally proportioned cartoon person will have a body that measures 7 1/2 "heads." This means that if the head is 1 cm (1/2 in.) tall, the whole body—including the head—will measure 8.5 cm (3 3/4 in.). To make your person look more heroic, lengthen the body to 8 "heads." If you want a female character to look very attractive, consider stretching her form to 9 "heads." On the other hand, if you want your characters to be cuter, cuddlier, and more appealing, shrink the bodies and increase the size of the heads. The characters in Charles Schulz's strip *Peanuts*, are about 2 1/2 "heads" tall. The *Rugrats* kids are about 2 "heads."

Use short, angular lines to draw male figures. Use long curves to draw adult women. Use gentle curves to draw kids.

Make sure the characteristics you give to your 'toon people enhance the cartoon's joke. If the joke has nothing to do with the character's personality, keep his or her look neutral. Unnecessary information will take away from the joke.

Face Facts

You already know how expressive faces can be. Use these great tips to really get your own cartoon faces to say what they mean before your characters even say a word.

When drawing faces, think about **eye position**. Eyes that are set close together or above the center of the head make your character look mean and unintelligent. Eyes that are placed farther apart convey a bright, innocent, sweet look.

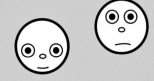

The **shape of the eyes** also makes a big difference. By changing the shape and size, you can make your character look naïve, sleepy, angry, surprised, dull, annoyed, sad, bored, or curious.

Adding **eyebrows** makes the eyes even more expressive. Experiment with different lines, angles, and sizes to see what effect you get.

Mouths also add expression and personality to your characters. Play around with their shapes. Mix and match different eyes, noses, and mouths to create entirely new characters.

Tips from the Pros

Not sure how to get the look you want? Keep a mirror handy! Test out a bunch of your own facial expressions. See if you can get the same look in your characters by copying what you see.

Add **hair** only after the rest of the head and face is complete. Think of the hair as part of the characters' clothing.

Drawing Animals

Most cartoon animals are *anthropomorphic*. The term anthropomorphic comes from the two Latin words that mean "human" and "shaped." This means that they look and act like humans. Think Mickey Mouse, Snoopy, Garfield.

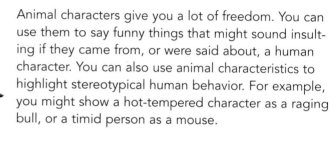

Animal characters give you a lot of freedom. You can use them to say funny things that might sound insulting if they came from, or were said about, a human character. You can also use animal characteristics to highlight stereotypical human behavior. For example, you might show a hot-tempered character as a raging bull, or a timid person as a mouse.

Great Moments in Cartoon History I

Walter Lantz and his new bride were enjoying the peace and quiet of their honeymoon, when they heard "Rat-a-tat-tat! Rat-a-tat-tat!" It was an unusually loud and persistent woodpecker, and the sound was driving them crazy! Never one to waste an opportunity, Lantz converted the pesky critter into a cartoon character with a singularly annoying personality. His name? Woody Woodpecker.

ANIMAL RULES

When drawing animals, follow the same rules that you use for humans. Create shtick by exaggerating personality characteristics. S-t-r-e-t-c-h physical traits, such as a duck's bill or a rabbit's long ears. Exaggerate emotion. Add clothing and props. Then set your creation free.

MIX IT UP!

You can mix animal and human traits to good effect. Let your doggy character sometimes behave like a typical dog. For example, she may be prone to chasing squirrels. Then have her behave like a human. For example, continuing on her way to school.

MAKING IT MOVE

In real life, people don't stay still. Getting movement into your cartoon characters is one more way to make them more interesting and eye-catching.

Drawing characters in motion means that sometimes you will have to draw them from different angles. For example, if your character is walking, you might want to show her from the side. At first, you may find it hard to show your characters in different positions. The key is practice.

BEGIN WITH THE FACE

Show your character face-on. Then show the face looking up, then down. Turn the face to one side. Look at the pictures below to give you an idea of how these pictures might look.

If you have trouble doing this, study a friend's head from different positions. What parts can you see? What parts are not visible at all, or only partially visible?

Once you have drawn your character from several angles, use the drawings as models to copy when you put together actual cartoons. Try and use at least two different face versions in each cartoon. With some practice, you will be able to draw your characters from any angle as easily as you can draw the full-front face.

BODY MECHANICS

Hands and feet are important to cartoonists. The hands show emotion and add action. The feet tell something about your character, and they "ground" the character, making him seem "solid."

Look at your own hand to see the basic relationships between the fingers. Practice drawing pictures of hands pointing, making a "stop!" gesture, holding an object, and making a fist. These gestures are all used often in cartooning.

To show the back of the hand, add fingernail shapes and knuckle lines to the basic hand shape. To show the palm, add a curved line at the base of the thumb. Remember to make the middle finger the longest, with the other fingers sloping down on both sides. Lines beside the hand indicate motion.

When you draw feet, add solid shoes that root your character in the ground. Make sure the feet are big enough so your character does not look like he or she will topple over. Practice drawing the shoes from different angles: straight on, from the side, or kicking.

Tips from the Pros

You can simplify quite a bit and still get a great effect. Many cartoonists only use three fingers and a thumb to create believable hands or paws. This "shorthand" works because the third and fourth fingers usually move together.

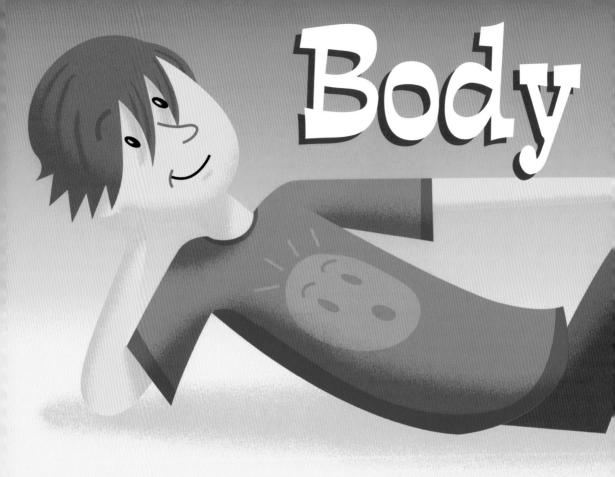

Body

Is your character happy or sad? Aggressive or timid? Stubborn or ashamed? The face can say a lot about these emotions, but so can the body. Think about what gestures you can add and what positions you can put your characters into to convey information.

Language

Tips from the Pros

Actions can also be very simple or subdued. Rolling eyes is an action. Yawning is an action. Even a character snoozing on the sofa is a character in action. The trick is to avoid people that stand around doing nothing, panel after panel.

WHAT WOULD IT SAY ABOUT YOUR CHARACTER IF SHE WERE...

- leaning towards someone while speaking, and pointing?
- strutting?
- crossing her arms across her chest?
- hanging her head?
- leaning back while being spoken to, and holding up her hand?
- standing with both hands on her hips?
- pulling at her hair?

139

Adding Action

Your characters aren't zombies, unless they are, well, zombies. So they can't just stand there. They've got to skip, cower, dance, huddle, wave, throw, fall, lounge, kiss, eat, spy, beg, hide, or otherwise get active. And you have to draw them doing it.

Before you begin your drawing, plan what your characters are going to do. Are they playing catch? If so, who is throwing, and who is catching? From what angle will you see the characters? Will the angle change in each panel?

Study each action. Choose the exact moment you would like to portray. If your character is throwing a ball, for example, do you want to show the wind up, the release, or the ball flying toward the target?

Once you decide what you want to show, do some research. Look at yourself in a mirror performing the action, watch friends in action, or find pictures in a magazine or newspaper that show the desired action. Make sure you study the pose from the same angle you intend to show it.

Try and capture the basic lines of the pose with a stick figure, drawn with solid hands and feet. Erase and redraw the lines until you feel they look right. Then use your stick figure as a guide when you draw your "real" character.

A Matter of Some GRAVITY

All objects that have mass also have a center of gravity. The center of gravity is the imaginary line that "pins" an object to the Earth. When objects (or people) topple, it is because the center of gravity is—oops!—not centered. Try this experiment to see for yourself.

1 Stand with both feet on the ground. Your center of gravity is running straight down through the top of your head into the ground beneath you.

2 Lift one foot and put it out in front of you like you are about to take a step. Do you feel yourself falling forward?

That is because as your foot moves outward from your body, your center of gravity shifts outward too. The rest of your mass will try to accommodate the shift by falling forward. You better put your foot down fast!

Cartoon characters also have centers of gravity. If they are not drawn with their centers of gravity correctly placed, they will look like they are about to fall over.

TIMBER*!!!*

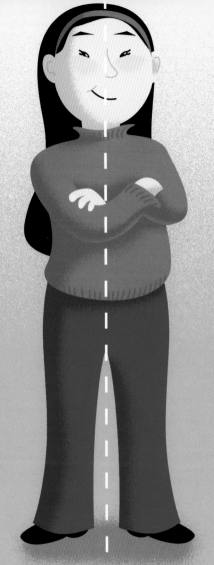

Luckily, it's easy to prevent toppling cartoons. When you position stationary characters, draw them so that about half of their bodies are on each side of their midline. Phew! They are now stable and in balance.

If you want to convey a sense of motion, however, draw your characters out of balance. A running character, for example, should have more than half of his body over his midline. The more speedily he is running, the more extreme the lean.

Draw your characters so that each half of their bodies is on one side of the center of gravity.

Setting the Scene

Now that you've got your characters ready, you need to place them in a scene. Drawing backgrounds can be very tricky, but a few tips will make your cartoons look top notch.

Change your point of view. To make a giant look taller, trees look more towering, or a flight of stairs look steeper, use a "worm's eye" view. That means you'll draw the scene as if you were looking directly up at it from the ground.

The opposite, a "bird's eye view," or a scene as seen from above, will make objects look smaller or more insignificant.

To add depth to your picture, draw close-up objects with more detail. Use bolder lines in the foreground, and broken lines in the background.

Highlight nearer or important objects by leaving a "halo" of white space around them.

You can use stereo-typical landscape features to create background. Think of a palm tree for a tropical island, a cactus for a desert, a snowman for "winter," or a black-board or desk to indicate school. Simplify these features so they don't take away from your central action or punch line.

Make objects appear farther away by drawing them smaller than the rest of the scene.

Use a "close up" to empha-size important emotions or objects.

145

Cartoon Shortcuts

Over the years, cartoonists have developed a kind of visual language to indicate some basic emotions or actions. By using these "shortcuts," you can spiff up your cartoon without too much effort.

SPEECH BALLOON
use for dialogue

THOUGHT BALLOON
use for thoughts

STATES OF MIND:
EXCITEMENT/CONFUSION/DISTRESS

EXCLAMATION OR
SOUND EFFECT BALLOON

BRIGHT IDEA

IMPACT

MUSICAL SOUNDS

HARD, DIRECT SOUNDS

SHRILL OR DISTURBING SOUNDS

MOTION
wobble lines

HEAT

MOTION
speed and direction

DIZZY

SLEEPING

CRYING

LOVE

ANGER

FEAR

147

Creating *the* Gag

You've created your characters. You've set the scene. Now all you need is a punch line. Coming up with jokes is hard for most people. Coming up with funny jokes is even harder. According to the experts, the only way to be sure of having a good idea is to have lots of them! Most will get tossed out, but the few that survive will be really funny.

OBSERVE... THEN TWIST

Cartoonists, like other humorists, get most of their ideas from studying people. Many keep notebooks to jot down ideas as they occur to them. They watch people everywhere: on the bus, at the supermarket, walking down the street. They also listen to how people speak, and the common expressions people use.

But cartoonists don't just draw what they observe. They add twists that make the observations funny and fresh. Coming up with the twists takes practice and skill.

Great Moments in Cartoon History II

Mort Walker, who created the classic comic strip *Beetle Bailey*, needed to deliver seven comic strips to the publisher each week. As a rule, he and his staff wrote 50—and discarded all but the seven best!

Add a Twist

Try some of the methods the pros use to develop your own twisted jokes.

1 Make a list of expressions people use everyday. Then think about a situation where these same words might seem funny. Try drawing a scene using some of these expressions to get you started:

- Have a nice day.
- Did you do your homework?
- What's for dinner?
- Two-for-one sale.
- You snooze, you lose.

HAVE AN ICE DAY!

2 Think of a common expression, then change a word for one with a similar sound, but a different meaning. Illustrate the result.

3 Think of some common scenes or events. For example, a family eating dinner, students in a classroom, a celebrity surrounded by cameras. What unexpected caption could you add to this familiar scene?

When back-to-school shopping lists and grocery lists get mixed up.

4 Find a picture in a magazine, like the one below. Think of your own hilarious captions to go with it.

Did you remember to turn off your stereo before we left?

...and Twist Some More

5 **Try "switching."** Find a cartoon or comic strip that you think is funny. Change one or two elements of the cartoon to create a completely original one based on the same idea.

6 **Train your visual sense.** First, imagine a scene, such as Goldilocks sitting down to eat some porridge. Picture it vividly. What details could be exaggerated for funny effect? How can you use this scene to create a great sight gag? Try to come up with a cartoon that has no text at all.

7 **Brainstorm using word association.** Start with a single word, such as "dog." Write down a list of everything that the word dog reminds you of. For example: teeth, tail, bowl, bone, dig, puppy, walking the dog, dog-sitting, roll over. Keep writing until an idea sparks in your mind. Sometimes, the way two or more of the words on your list interact will give you an idea. For example, the words "tail" and "bowl" might spark a picture of the dog bowl with a tail, which is wagging as the pet owner pours food into it.

8 **Make a chart** with three columns. In the first column, list the names of objects, types of people, and animals. In the second column, make a list of actions. In the third column, list settings. At random, choose 1 word from each column. Try and create a cartoon using these three elements.

Column A	Column B	Column C
wolf	dancing	forest
refrigerator	rolling	classroom
pencil sharpener	falling	gym

9

Doodle a familiar object, say, a hammer. Add kooky features to it, like an on/off switch.

Laff-Riot Recipes V

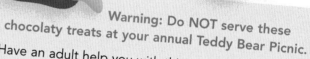

BEAR CLAW CANDIES

You'll Need

500 mL (2 cups) chocolate chips

250 mL (1 cup) whole cashews*

* If you have a nut allergy, you can substitute candy pieces or candy corn.

You'll Also Need

measuring cup

microwaveable bowl or small pot

mixing spoon • cookie sheet

spoon • waxed paper

YIELD: About 10 bear claws

PREP. TIME: 15 minutes, plus cooling time

Warning: Do NOT serve these chocolaty treats at your annual Teddy Bear Picnic.

1. Have an adult help you with this step. Melt the chocolate chips over low heat in the small pot on the stove. If you have a microwave, you can melt the chips in the microwaveable bowl.

2. Stir the melted chips with the spoon until the chocolate is smooth. Be careful not to burn. Remove from heat.

3. Lay a sheet of waxed paper on the cookie sheet.

4. Using a spoon, drop the melted chocolate into rounded blobs onto the waxed paper. Each blob should be about 5 cm (2 in.) wide. These will be your bear paws.

5. While the chocolate is still warm, place three or four cashews, curved side down, onto one side of the paw. One half of the cashew should be in the chocolate, with half hanging off. These are your "claws." Allow to cool.

Being funny is such hard work! When you need a break from being so darn hilarious, hightail it to the kitchen. You'll have fun and stimulate your creative juices when you make these creative—and delicious!—snacks.

MOOSE DROPPINGS

You'll Need

225 g (8 oz.) semisweet chocolate, in chunks or chips

185 mL (3/4 cups) sweetened, condensed milk

250 mL (1 cup) total of any of the assorted (mix or match to taste): raisins, chopped nuts, your favorite cereal, mini marshmallows

You'll Also Need

measuring cups • mixing spoon

microwaveable bowl or small pot

spoon • waxed paper • cookie sheet

What do chocolate moose produce? What "elks" but these incredible edibles?

1 Combine chocolate and condensed milk in microwaveable bowl or pot. Microwave about 1 minute. Or melt in small pot, stirring over low heat on stove. Remove from heat.

2 Add raisins, nuts, cereal, and/or marshmallows. Mix to combine.

3 Line a cookie sheet with waxed paper. Using a spoon, drop mixture in small clumps onto sheet. Allow to cool. Serve with milk. Yum.

YIELD: about 10 moose droppings, depending on size

PREP. TIME: 15 minutes, plus cooling time

ANIMATING
Your Cartoons

Your drawings are so terrific, they almost seem like they can move by themselves. Wouldn't it be cool if you really could see them in action? It's easier than you might think to make your own animated cartoons. When you've got the basics of showing your characters in action, it's only a short step to making moving pictures of your own.

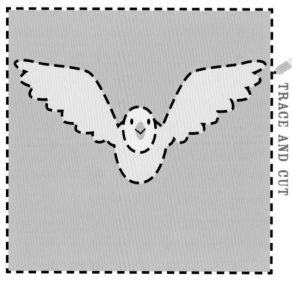

TRACE AND CUT

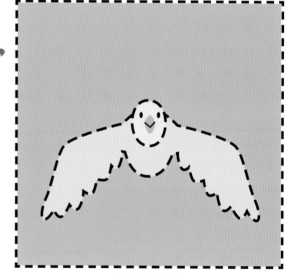

BIRDIE 1

BIRDIE 2

Flying Birdie FLIPBOOK

Once you get the hang of this very simple two-page flipbook,
you can draw your own two-part actions to create an original mini-flipbook.

YOU'LL NEED

drawing materials

two sheets of paper

scissors

stapler

1 Trace Birdie 1 and its box outline onto the first sheet of paper. Color the bird in as desired. Cut out around the surrounding box.

2 Trace Birdie 2 and its box outline onto the second sheet of paper. Color the same way as you colored Birdie 1. Cut out.

3 Staple the two pictures together along the lefthand edge, one on top of the other.

4 Quickly flip back and forth between the two pictures. It's magic! The birdie flaps its wings and flies!

WHY DOES IT WORK?

What makes the birdie appear to fly? The trick is a quirk of our eyes called persistence of vision. Your eye and brain can retain a visual impression for about $1/30$th of a second. If you flip the pages of your birdie book back and forth fast enough, your brain can hang onto the first image long enough to fool itself into seeing a single smooth motion.

Birdie in a Cage CRAFT

This nifty old-fashioned toy also shows persistence of vision (see page 155) at work.

(see page 155)

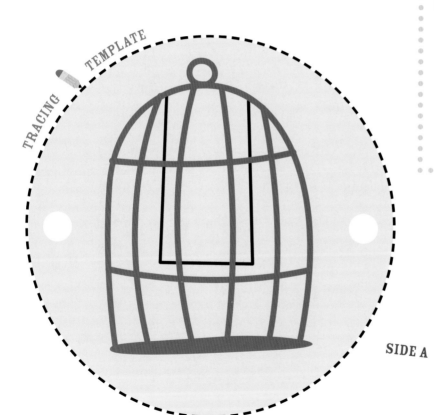

TRACING TEMPLATE

SIDE A

156

1. Cut out a circle from the cardboard measuring 10 cm (4 in.) across. (You can trace the circle on page 156.)

2. Use the hole punch to make two holes in the cardboard as shown.

3. Copy or trace the picture of the birdcage onto one side of the circle.

4. Turn the circle over. The birdcage on the back should now be upside-down.

5. In the center of the circle, copy or trace the picture of the bird. Color.

6. Pull a rubber band through one hole. Slip one loop through the other and pull through to form a knot. Repeat with the other rubber band in the other hole.

7. Twist the rubber bands back and forth rapidly. The circle should spin back and forth between them. And look! The birdie is magically in the cage!

This toy, called a thaumatrope, was invented in 1825.

Remember to turn the cage upside down before flipping to draw the bird.

SIDE B

157

More **FLIPBOOK** Animation

The Flying Birdie and the Birdie in a Cage are examples of very simple animation. You can make more ambitious flipbooks simply by using more images. The best way to create the images is by using a thick pad of drawing paper. Here's how.

YOU'LL NEED

a thick pad of paper—
say, 100 sheets
(a small notepad is best)

drawing materials

1 Plan your action. Begin with a simple series, such as man walking down the street. Start in pencil so that you can erase if you need to.

2 On the top sheet of paper, draw the man standing in the bottom right corner.

3 On the second sheet, right below the first, draw the same man putting out his left foot. Make the right arm swing in time with the left foot.

4 On the third sheet of the pad, draw the man again, this time below the second picture. Draw the man putting down his left foot, and picking up his right foot. Draw the left arm swinging forward and the left arm moving back.

5 Repeat the sequence from step two. After you have completed a few pictures, check your work. To do so, hold the booklet in your left hand. Then, using the thumb of your right hand, rapidly flip the pages of the book. You should be able to see your little guy in motion!

6 As your skill increases, you can add more complicated actions—two kids playing catch; a dog chasing a squirrel up a tree; two people break-dancing. The only limit to your designs is your imagination!